Y0-BSS-145

AN AMERICAN DREAM

CLARENCE ADAMS

An American Dream

The Life of an African American Soldier and POW Who Spent Twelve Years in Communist China

Edited by DELLA ADAMS & LEWIS H. CARLSON

University of Massachusetts Press   Amherst and Boston

LC 2007004224
ISBN 978-1-55849-595-1 (paper); 594-4 (library cloth)
Designed by Richard Hendel
Set in Quadraat and Mrs. Eaves by dix!
Printed and bound by The Maple-Vail Book Manufacturing Group

Library of Congress Cataloging-in-Publication Data

Adams, Clarence, 1929–1999.
An American dream : the life of an African American soldier and
POW who spent twelve years in communist China / Clarence Adams;
edited by Della Adams and Lewis H. Carlson.
p.   cm.
Includes bibliographical references.
ISBN 978-1-55849-595-1 (pbk. : alk. paper)
ISBN 978-1-55849-594-4 (cloth : alk. paper)
1. Korean War, 1950–1953—Prisoners and prisons, American.   2. Adams,
Clarence, 1929–1999.   3. Prisoners of war—United States—Biography.
4. Prisoners of war—Korea (North)—Biography.   5. Prisoners of war—China—
Biography.   I. Adams, Della, 1939–   II. Carlson, Lewis H.   III. Title.
DS921.A33 2007
951.904′27—dc22
[B]   2007004224

British Library Cataloguing in Publication data are available.

This book is published with the support and cooperation
of the William Joiner Center for the Study of War and Social
Consequences, University of Massachusetts Boston, and
the William Joiner Foundation, Boston, Massachusetts.

FRONTISPIECE
Clarence Adams, age 17.

What happens to a dream deferred?

Does it dry up

like a raisin in the sun?

Or fester like a sore—

and then run?

Does it stink like rotten meat?

Or crust and sugar over

like a syrupy sweet?

LANGSTON HUGHES

I still have a dream,

a dream deeply rooted in the

American Dream . . .

I have a dream that one day every

valley shall be exalted . . .

MARTIN LUTHER KING JR.

CONTENTS

ILLUSTRATIONS

Throughout his life, Clarence Cecil "Skippy" Adams exhibited self-reliance, ambition, ingenuity, courage, and a commitment to learning. In short, he exemplified those character traits his fellow countrymen equated with the successful pursuit of the American Dream. Unfortunately, for an African American coming of age in the 1930s and 1940s, such attributes counted for little, especially if he lived in the South.

Clarence Adams had another strike against him. In 1953, after spending thirty-three months as a POW during the Korean War, he chose not to return to his homeland; instead, he went to China, where he spent the next twelve years of his life. The American media, military, and government referred to him as a turncoat, a collaborator, and a Communist. After he returned to the United States in 1966, the House Un-American Activities Committee accused him of "disrupting the morale of the American fighting forces in Vietnam and inciting revolution in the U.S." Adams vigorously denied these charges, explaining: "I went to China because I was looking for freedom, a way out of poverty, and to be treated like a human being, instead of something sub-human. I never belonged to the Communist Party, I never became a Chinese citizen, and in no way did I betray my country."

Was Clarence Adams telling the truth? I believe he was. He never joined the Communist Party in China or anywhere else. Nor did he betray his country in any legal sense. He divulged no secrets; indeed, none of the twenty-one liberated American POWs who chose in 1953 to live in China knew any. Were these men turncoats? That is a matter of interpretation. Under the terms of the truce agreement ending the Korean War hostilities, liberated prisoners had the right to go to any country that would take them. Of course, American negotiators were thinking of the thousands of Communist prisoners who did not want to return to North Korea or the People's Republic of China, not of their own countrymen. Adams did make a controversial broadcast during the Vietnam War, urging African American troops to fight for their own freedom at home rather than for someone else's rights in a country they had never heard of, but he insisted he was addressing only black troops, not the entire U.S. military. In Adams's mind, if the United States had been as concerned with ending racism at home as it was with defeating communism abroad, he would have had no reason to seek a new life in another country.

One must place Clarence Adams's story, and that of the other twenty non-repatriates, within the perspective of the times. It was the height of the Cold War, McCarthyism, and what Richard Hofstadter called "the Paranoid Style in American Politics." Just five years after having won a second global war to make the world safe for democracy, Americans saw themselves once again under siege. This time it was the Communists who had to be stopped; but the three-year "police action" in Korea, which cost the lives of more than 36,000 Americans, ended in a frustrating stalemate.

Against this backdrop, how does one explain twenty-one American soldiers refusing repatriation in 1953, along with the hundreds of other POWs who stood accused of collaborating with their captors? Were these men any different from the likes of Alger Hiss, who allegedly gave state secrets to the Soviets, or Julius and Ethel Rosenberg, who in 1953 were executed for the same offense? Or were the twenty-one "turncoats" victims of a diabolical new form of mind control called "brainwashing," administered by a heinous enemy of the mysterious East?

The American media had no problem accusing the twenty-one non-repatriates of a plethora of shortcomings: they were guilty of poor family histories, low intelligence, homosexuality, weak ethnicity, psychological malfunctions; they were also condemned for falling in love with foreign women, betraying fellow prisoners, and collaborating with the enemy. The media, however, never explored possible rents in the American social fabric, although racism and the search for educational and economic opportunities were certainly the primary motivation for Clarence Adams and the other two African Americans who refused repatriation.

I never met Clarence Adams, at least not face-to-face, but in 1953, as a college sophomore safely deferred from military service, I certainly learned about him and the other alleged turncoats through the media. I was too young, naïve, and secure to worry about such matters, although the United States was then deep in the throes of Joseph McCarthy's four-year crusade to rid the country of real and imagined Communists. Not even when a favorite junior high school teacher in my hometown of Muskegon, Michigan, was fired for having written a utopian novel, or when the University of Michigan sacked three professors for refusing to sign a loyalty oath, did it register on me that an unhealthy paranoia was sweeping the country.

Forty-six years later I wrote Clarence Adams requesting an interview for a book I was writing on American Korean War POWs. I was too late. He had just died. But his daughter Della answered my letter and was kind enough to grant me an interview, parts of which appeared in my book, *Remembered Prisoners of a Forgotten War*. Several years later she asked me if I might be interested in helping her put together the story of her father's life. This book is the result.

The sources for the Clarence Adams who emerges in this book are many. Foremost are the many hours of audiotapes he recorded, his copious notes, and a partial memoir. He had also written an earlier autobiography while living in China but decided against trying to take it with him in 1966 when he and his Chinese family returned to the United States. It was the height of the Cultural Revolution, and he and his wife, Lin, had come under suspicion. They feared that if the authorities discovered what he had written, they would not be allowed to leave China, or even worse, that they would be severely punished. A Swedish journalist and friend agreed to take the manuscript with him when he left for Sweden. Unfortunately, both he and the autobiography have long since disappeared. Many of the gaps in Adams's life have been filled in by the two people who knew him best: wife Lin, who has also recorded many of her memories, and daughter Della, who spent many, many days, and not a few nights, talking endlessly with her father about his life. Also helpful have been friends who knew Clarence Adams in Memphis, in the military, and in the prisoner of war camps. In addition, many newspaper and magazine articles quoted him, though often out of context, and sometimes after changing his words to fit the tenor of the times.

What emerges from these sources is a man of tremendous spirit and determination. The tapes also capture something the printed word cannot: a rich and abiding laughter and an enviable talent for oral storytelling. Adams was fun-loving, gregarious, generous, and sincerely concerned about the human condition. He was also irrepressible, feisty, and marched to his own drummer. He was often a square peg in a round hole, who had no difficulty finding trouble on two continents. Unquestionably, a deep-rooted anger also motivated many of his actions. A half-century ago novelist James Baldwin wrote, "To be a Negro in America, and to be relatively conscious, is to be in a perpetual rage." Individual and institutional racism certainly fueled Adams's anger, but he also felt unworthy and rejected because of an unstable relationship with his mother, who, at least subconsciously, saw his illegitimate birth as a precipitating factor in her own unhappy life.

Above all, Clarence Adams was a survivor. Whether growing up on the mean streets of a rigidly segregated Memphis, fighting on the front lines in Korea, surviving as a POW that first deadly winter of 1950–51 when more than 50 percent of his fellow prisoners died, educating himself in a strange, unfamiliar country, or after returning to an America that wanted to try him for treason, Clarence Adams never lost his will to succeed. Without question, his life contains much of what Americans have traditionally admired in their heroes; but he was also a black man who, at the height of the McCarthy era, defiantly chose a Communist nation over his own country.

Americans who have been so quick to judge Clarence Adams must ask themselves a simple question: In spite of his obvious intelligence and great desire to improve himself, would he have had the kind of educational and professional opportunities afforded him in China had he remained in his native Memphis? Eventually, perhaps, but certainly not in 1953.

My father, Clarence Adams, was a man of conviction who lived his life without compromise, regardless of the consequences. Even before he passed on September 17, 1999, it was always my dream that the story of this extraordinary African American, who had lived such an uncommon and fascinating life, could be told to the world. My father many times attempted to put his life down on paper, hoping that in doing so he would correct the distortions and fabrications that surrounded his decision in 1953 not to return home from a North Korean prison camp, but to create a new life for himself in the People's Republic of China. These misrepresentations and untruths surfaced again in 1966, when he decided to return to the United States, bringing his Chinese wife and two young children with him.

Above all, my father wanted Americans to understand why he went to China. He did not adhere to some abstract or subversive political ideology. To the contrary, he based his decision solely on his inalienable right to live as a human being. America denied him that right, whereas China assured him open and equal opportunities. It was just that simple.

I also had a selfish reason for wanting his story told. Through the process of gathering notes, letters, tape recordings, photographs, newspaper articles, and official documents, as well as reliving our countless conversations, I fervently hoped to reconnect with him. My father had been snatched from me when he died in my arms as I drove frantically down the interstate trying to get him to the hospital. He had suffered an acute emphysema attack and was having extreme difficulties breathing. When my three attempts to call 911 failed to reach anyone, I had no choice but to drive him myself. His last words to me were, "Della, I'm not going to make it." The trauma and unrelenting pain of that night have never left me. The public telling of his story is a very personal attempt to come to terms with his death and to mitigate some of my emotional suffering.

My father was a great storyteller. Listeners were simply spellbound when he described his experiences growing up in rigidly segregated Memphis, of being a combat infantryman and POW in North Korea, an expatriate in China, and, later, an accused witness before the House Un-American Activities Committee. I was certainly one of his most avid listeners, and I greatly regret that he was unable to finish writing his autobiography, even though the words in this book are certainly his.

Quite by accident, I came in contact with Lewis Carlson, who called me shortly after my father's death. At the time he was working on a book about Korean War POWs. Initially he had wanted to interview my father, but after learning of his death, he asked to talk with me. At first, I was not receptive because I knew how strongly my father would have felt about having someone else tell his story. He had suffered several bad experiences when people he trusted took that story and twisted it for their own use. Something in Lew's voice, however, told me that it was going to be all right. After reading his *Remembered Prisoners of a Forgotten War*, in which he faithfully recounted my words about my father, I felt that he was the right person with whom to collaborate in putting together this book.

Throughout our turbulent years in China and, later, in the United States, my father was the focal point for all members of our family. After losing him, all of us experienced great difficulty in finding our own way. His unrelenting determination to succeed and great personal courage would have been difficult for anyone to live up to. My brother in particular had a hard time, but even as a daughter, I was expected to show great bravery. I remember when I was about eight years old running home from school crying after an older boy threatened to beat me up because of my mixed race. My father came home early from work to deal with the problem. He stood on the porch and told me in no uncertain terms that if I did not go back and fight that nasty boy he was going to whip me. I was more afraid of disappointing my father than of getting beaten up by any boy. So I fought him and I lost. Still, I learned a valuable lesson that day. If I had not overcome my fear, I would have gone through life being afraid and allowing people to intimidate me. Recognizing my newfound confidence, my father taught me how to defend myself. I never lost another fight, and I had many.

My father and I could talk about anything. I especially admired his understanding and compassion for the common man. Nevertheless, we had our disagreements. My mother often accused me of being just like him: stubborn and opinionated. Our personalities were very similar, and we were the best of buddies when we got along. When we disagreed about something, however, we had some very heated arguments, with neither of us backing down. But we also enjoyed these verbal skirmishes, especially when these debates occurred over a bottle of Old Grand Dad.

· · · · · ★ · · · · ·

I never doubted that my father loved me, but he was not an openly affectionate man. He rarely hugged me or told me he loved me. In this he was like most men of his generation. A few months before his death we became much closer and our conversations became more frequent. I really felt that we had come to an understanding on certain issues on which we had previously disagreed. He even told me that he was proud of the fact that I was just as hardheaded and single-minded as he was. Those words meant everything to me, and they convinced me that we certainly needed more time together. It is my hope that the pages of this book will help fulfill that need.

AN AMERICAN DREAM

CHAPTER ONE

Skippy: The Formative Years

So many African Americans migrated north to Memphis in the 1890s that by the end of the nineteenth century, they made up approximately half of its 100,000 inhabitants. According to historian David M. Tucker, they came "for political freedom as well as the educational and economic opportunities of a city [and] three-fourths of the incoming black immigrants were Mississippi-born."[1] Clarence Adams's grandparents were part of this migration pursuing the American Dream of economic opportunity. The women worked as domestics and pushed their children into and through the segregated public schools, while the men found work as gardeners and in the railroad yards and lumber mills.[2]

There were more unsavory opportunities to be found in gambling, saloons, and prostitution. By the time Clarence Adams was born in 1929, a small black middle class had emerged in Memphis, consisting of educators like his father, as well as businessmen, physicians, funeral directors, bankers, and journalists for Memphis's two black newspapers. But all lived under the rigid political machine controlled by Boss E. H. Crump, who ruled Memphis, black and white, with an iron fist from 1909 until his death in 1954.

In 1955 a woman named Virginia Pasley wrote a book called 21 Stayed in which she tried to explain why each of the twenty-one American POWs decided not to return home at the end of the Korean War. When she came to my story, she insisted I was "an informant to the Chinese on activities of loyal Americans held prisoner." This was, of course, untrue, and so was her patronizing comment that I had been a child "with no friends, . . . a delicate kid who tried to the limits of his capacities." She also wrote that I had "made a bitter statement at Panmunjom about race prejudice and segregation." She was half right. I did

> I might not have known what China was really like before I went there, but I certainly knew what life was like for blacks in America, and especially in Memphis.
> — Clarence Adams

> You have a bunch of niggers teaching social equality, stirring up social hatred [in Memphis]. . . . I am not going to tolerate a bunch of niggers spreading racial hatred and running things their way. Tell them Mr. Crump said so.
> — E. H. Crump, Memphis political boss, 1939

make such a statement, but it was truth and not bitterness that made me say that it was racism at home rather than Chinese propaganda that inspired my decision. She also quoted an unnamed Memphis teacher who allegedly said, "Those words were not Skippy's. He did not leave Memphis with any of those feelings. The average colored boy faces up to the segregation and accepts it and goes on about his business."[3] Such a statement was an insult to any thinking African American and certainly stood in sharp contrast to why I went to China.

..... ★ .....

I will never know the reasons why my mother never forgave me for being her son. Even as she lay dying in a Memphis hospital from cancer of the uterus and kidney failure in March 1977, she rejected me. She was semi-delirious and drifting in and out of consciousness. When I walked into the room, the attending nurse gently touched her shoulder and said, "Mrs. Peoples, your son is here to see you." My mother opened her eyes, looked up, and said, "Son? What son? I don't have a son."

I never met my father. He died before I could ever talk to him. In fact, for a long time no one ever told me who my father was. What little I now know about him I learned from my mother's brother, King Adams, after I returned to the United States from China in 1966. He told me I was born on January 4, 1929, in a boardinghouse on South Front Street where my mother, Gladys Adams, whom everyone called Toosie, secretly stayed while awaiting my birth.

My father's name was Charles Holmes. He was born in Duck Hill, Mississippi, one of Burrell and Isabella Wilkerson Campbell's eleven children. His father died in a train accident in 1885, after which his mother moved the family to Memphis, where literally thousands of Mississippi blacks came during the late nineteenth and early twentieth centuries looking for a better way of life. In Memphis she worked at a variety of domestic jobs to keep the family intact. She was a great believer in education and insisted that her children go as far as possible in school. My father was an educated man and supposedly a brilliant orator. When he met my mother, he was a bachelor and an assistant principal at Booker T. Washington High School in Memphis, where she was an eighteen-year-old student. For reasons that are not clear, she went to his home one afternoon, and soon after found herself pregnant. Pregnancy outside of marriage was much more scandalous in the 1920s than today, and Charles offered to marry Toosie, but she and her family turned him down. He was subsequently fired from his position at the school, and after a year of trying to run the Holmes School of Music in Memphis, he returned to Duck Hill. He never married, and died there of pneumonia in 1933. My father had a very famous sister named Lucie Campbell who also taught at Booker T. Washington High School. In fact, the two of them were living together on Saxon Avenue at the time my mother became pregnant. Lucie Campbell later became one of the nation's best-known gospel songwriters. When she died in 1963 at age seventy-seven, she left part of her estate to me because I was her closest living relative. Unfortunately, my mother refused to tell the estate attorneys where I could be located. At the time I was living in China and never heard about any of this, so all her money went to other relatives.[4]

Immediately after my birth I was taken to live with my mother's parents on Pillow Street in a neighborhood now called South Memphis. For years I thought my grandparents were my mother and father. Peter and Alice Wright Adams had moved to Memphis from Clarksdale, Mississippi, with a mule, a wagon, a pack of kids, and not much else.

Grandmother Adams was the backbone of the family because my grandfather was always on the go. They had thirteen children, eleven of whom survived. My mother was next to the youngest. Grandmother Adams was an amazingly hardworking woman, and she saw to it that her children always had a roof over their heads, clothes on their backs, and food on the table. She could do anything. She built their house pretty much by herself, and she did it so well that it lasted until 1996. She raised fruits and vegetables, took in washing from white people, and with her mule and wagon collected and sold scrap metal and junk.

Grandmother Adams called me Skippy because I was such a happy child while I lived with her and because I was always getting into mischief. The name Skippy stuck with me all through my childhood and even in the army, although when I was stationed in Japan, some of my buddies began calling me Fish or King Fish because I was a slick gambler who always beat them when we shot craps or played poker.

At the time there were few other houses in my grandparents' neighborhood, although later, after the city annexed the surrounding land, it became the site of Hamilton Elementary, Middle, and High School. My Uncle King Adams and his wife, Beatrice, lived in this same house with their two sons after my grandparents died, and after I returned from China in 1966 with Lin and our two children, Della and Louis. We also lived there for several months when my mother no longer wanted us living with her.

My earliest memory of my grandparents' house was of a large German shepherd named Flora, whom I rode like a horse. I also remember a dark, damp space underneath their propped-up house that only I could crawl in and out of easily. When grownups discovered that I was playing with a large snake under the house, they refused to kill it because, according to local superstition, a snake that befriends a child should not be harmed or the child will die. Uncle King caught the snake and carefully transported it to a nearby woods and let it go.

When I was four or five years old, I fell off the porch and slashed my head. In fact, I still have the scar. My grandfather picked me up and ran with me in his arms all the way to John Gaston Hospital, which was a good ten miles away, and Grandmother ran right alongside him. That's how strong they were and how much they loved me. They always made me feel special, and my years with them were undoubtedly the most joyful and secure of my life. Unfortunately, they both died when I was six years old.

I remember a lot of people coming to the house after the funeral. Among them was a young woman everyone called Toosie. She had occasionally come to the house and played with me, but that's all I knew about her. Somebody told me I now had to go live with her, and I started to cry, because I certainly did not want to leave my grandparents' house to go with somebody I didn't even know.

Toosie took me to her house, where I met a slim man named Fred Peoples and three little girls with big eyes, named Alice, Barbara, and Nellie (their last child, Kate, was not yet born). Only years later did I learn that Toosie was actually my mother. Initially, I thought Fred was my father. I also later learned that Toosie had not told Fred about me, so I guess I was somewhat of a surprise to him, and certainly an embarrassment for her when she had to bring me into their home.

Toosie worked at the White Rose Laundry. When she was young and all dressed up, she was indeed a pretty sight. She worked as a checker in the front, a job normally filled by a white woman. Fred worked as a sander at the Memphis Furniture Factory, but he also did yard work for Mrs. Johnson, the widow of Memphis banker R. O. Johnson. In exchange, Mrs. Johnson let our family rent two rooms in one of the three garages behind her house, known as the old Coward Place, for fifteen dollars a month. Fred and Toosie stayed in the upstairs room, which also doubled as a living room during the day. I shared a room downstairs with my half-sisters, which was also the kitchen. The room was far too small for all four of us, so with the permission of Mrs. Johnson, Fred knocked a hole in the kitchen wall and built in a box bed which protruded into an unused part of the garage. It was like sleeping in a small coffin, but it was warm and cozy.

I started wondering about my real father when nosy people in the neighborhood asked, "Hey, boy, who's your daddy?"

I'd get confused and say, "Fred's my daddy." I always called him Fred, never Daddy, and I always called my mother Toosie. She only allowed her daughters to call her Momma or Mother. Later in life she even insisted that her grandchildren call her Toosie, because she thought she was too young to be a grandmother. When I think back on all this, it does seem odd that I was the only one in the family who called Fred and Toosie by their first names. But as I got older, when these insensitive people would call me over to their front porches and ask, "Boy, who's your daddy?" I'd look at them like they were crazy. I'd get angry and ask, "What do you mean, who's my daddy? Fred's my daddy."

Then they'd say, "If that's true, why's your name Adams and not Peoples like your sisters'?"

I finally got the courage to ask my mother, "Is Fred my real daddy?" She slapped me across the face and yelled, "Don't you ever ask me that again." I did not, but when I was about fifteen, I asked an aunt of my mother's, whom we all called Sister, about my real father. She said, "I can't tell you anything 'cause if I do, your momma will kill me." Then I asked my Uncle King, and he told me, "Fred's not your daddy. One day you'll know about all this." He still was not ready to tell me the whole story, but by then I knew something was not right. I did not know the details, but I did know that Toosie was my real mother and that Fred was not my real father. I do not even look like my sisters, who all look like Fred. Frankly speaking, I also bear little resemblance to my real father. I look more like my mother. Her mother was half Indian and her father also had Indian blood. My grandmother had very long black hair and an Indian's complexion. My mother was light-skinned, but my real father was as black as coal.

All this uncertainty about my parentage led to a very bad relationship between my stepfather and me. At first I listened to and obeyed him, but now, in my teenage mind, I started thinking back on things I asked for but never got. When I wanted toys or a pair of shoes, I never got them, but my sisters always did. All my clothes were hand-me-downs from Mrs. Johnson's grandson, who was a year older than I. She would give Fred clothes her grandson had outgrown, and they would become my Christmas presents. My sisters got new clothes for every holiday. When I complained, my stepfather would give me a hug and say, "You're a boy. You don't need new things. Boys don't even

Clarence Adams's maternal grandparents, Peter Adams and Alice Wright Adams, holding Mary and Vivian, two of their thirteen children. Their daughter Gladys, Clarence Adams's mother, was born on November 10, 1910.

Gladys "Toosie" Adams at age 41.

Clarence Adams's father, Charles Holmes (second row, far left), in a 1927 Booker T. Washington High School faculty photo. Charles's sister Lucie E. Campbell-Williams, who composed over 100 gospel songs, is second from the right in the second row. Taken from G. P. Hamilton's Booker T. Washington High School, 1891–1927 (self-published, 1927).

want new things. You've got to be strong. This will make a man out of you." When he said things like this, I began to think back on all the times I had been denied things I thought I should have had, and, in my adolescent mind, I came to the conclusion, "That's because Fred's not my father."

White kids wore different clothes than black kids, so the black kids in the neighborhood laughed at Mrs. Johnson's grandson's hand-me-downs. These were the kinds of clothes rich British kids wore, including knickers that came down just below the knees, with long stockings. Black kids didn't wear things like that. When I went to school I looked like a little British boy, and everybody laughed at me. In response, I learned to fight. Then, when they laughed at me, I could at least beat them up.

Mrs. Johnson's house still stands, although it later became the best and most expensive restaurant in Memphis. It's called Justine's, and only rich white folks go there. My cousin Gilda Lee took me there once. She had plenty of money because her father, Colonel George Washington Lee, was a very

Clarence "Skippy" Adams at age 16.

The Coward Place, or Justine's, as it looks today.

successful writer, businessman, and Republican Party figure in Memphis. In fact, as head of the Republican Party of Tennessee when it was mostly a black party, he made a seconding speech at the Republican Convention in 1952 for the nomination of Senator Robert A. Taft. The bill for that dinner at Justine's came to over one hundred dollars, and I did not even like the food.

I often accompanied my stepfather to Mrs. Johnson's home, where he cut the grass, trimmed the bushes, and worked in the garden. Mrs. Johnson would sometimes call me into the house to do little jobs, like waxing the floors and polishing the brass railings. I remember once stealing a can of rattlesnake meat to see how it tasted. I thought to myself, "If rich people eat snake, I've got to try some." But I did not like it and threw it away. Rattlesnake meat was one of the few things rich people had that I did not want.

I had another strange experience with white people's food when I was eleven or twelve years old. I was wearing some old ragged play clothes and walking through this nice middle-class white neighborhood when an old woman, I think she was Italian, came out on her porch and said, "Hey, boy, come here. You want something to eat?" Well, I wasn't even hungry, but I was always curious about what white people ate. She said, "Come around to the back door." At that time, of course, blacks were not allowed to go in the front door of white houses. I went around to the back and she sat me down and brought me a glass of goat's milk, which I had never tasted. She set it in front of me, and I put it up to my nose. It didn't smell good, but she was watching me, so I had to take a sip. It was bitter. She said, "Go ahead and drink it. I'll be right back." When she left the room, I poured it out in the sink. When she got back, she asked me, "Do you want some more?" I told her, "Oh, no ma'am. No ma'am! It was good, but I don't want any more." I hurried up and got out of there. She really meant well. She just wanted to do something nice for a little hungry black kid. But I wasn't hungry. I was just curious — and greedy.

We did not eat like white people. We ate our own food, and as a result, black kids were stronger and healthier than most white kids. Our basic foods were greens, beans, peas, and cornbread. We ate a lot more vegetables than meat. Meat was only for Sunday, when we might have chicken or some kind of pork with gravy and rice. White people ate the best parts of the hog; we ate what was left. When I was a kid, we'd go to this Jewish butcher store, Le Belies, and they'd give us neck bones. I used to carry big grocery bags of neck bones home that I got for free. They were great for making soup. Of course, I'd be spitting out bones all day after eating that soup. We also ate chicken feet and chitlins, which are cooked pig intestines, but this kind of food made us strong.

We never let the fire go out in our big old kitchen stove, even in the summer. We'd buy wood and coal by the ton and keep it in the yard. In the winter we used coal, but in the summer it was wood. There was always something cooking on the stove, like beans or greens. I used to go to the Chickasaw Coal Yard and steal coal the trains dumped there. There was a fence around the coal yard, but there were always cracks in it. I'd haul my homemade wagon up to the fence, grab a stick, poke it through the fence, and fish out slack coal, which were little pieces that burned well. I'd get a wagonful, take it home, and do it again the next night. I'd keep doing this until I had enough coal to last maybe a month. I also picked up empty wood packing crates that had been left along the tracks after being unloaded. I'd do this at night, so I suppose this was one time when it helped to be black.

I did this on my own because my mother and stepfather would never have allowed me to steal anything. Oh, yeah, I learned to steal all on my own. I really considered it borrowing. I planned to pay the coal yard back if I ever got rich enough, but of course I never did.

I had lots of chores growing up. We did not have any grass around the garage where we lived, just dirt, so I had to sweep the dirt with a broom. Inside the house, I had to scrub the wooden floors with a brush until they were white.

It was also my job to scour the pots and pans, although my sisters washed the dishes. I also had to wash my stepfather's work clothes and our family quilts by hand on a scrub-board in a tub. That's why they say rub-a-dub-dub.

When I turned seven, I began attending the nearest all-black school. Our books were hand-me-downs from the city's white schools. My report card from third grade shows that I got A's and B's in math, science, and shop, but a red F+ for conduct. I did well enough in school when I wanted to, but I was often bored. Sometimes I would threaten my sister Alice, who always got good grades, and make her do my homework. The teacher sent notes home with me complaining about my constant talking and joking in class. Of course, the notes never made it home to Toosie.

Black kids played mostly in the streets because we did not have access to parks or swimming pools like whites did. If we wanted to swim, we had to use the creeks, bayous, and the backwaters of the Mississippi River. When I was just a little kid, maybe eight or nine years old, two of my uncles taught me how to swim in Nonconnah Creek. They told me to jump in, but I was afraid. So they grabbed my hands and feet, swung me back and forth, and threw me in the water. I landed in the middle of the creek. I thought they were going to jump in and rescue me, but they just stood on the bank. When I realized they were not going to help me, I started splashing around and beating my arms. I managed to kick my way out of there. After that I was willing to do anything in water, including diving out of trees into the Wolf River.

Black kids also made their own toys. White kids always seemed to have big shiny bicycles, but I made my own bike. I went to the junkyard and found bits and pieces of old bikes. I discovered a wheel here, a handlebar there, and a pedal somewhere else. When I had enough scraps, I built myself a bike. We also made our own wagons and scooters. I remember finding some old skates, taking the wheels off, nailing them onto a piece of wood, and making a skateboard. We were really very inventive. Nobody ever bought us any toys. We learned a lot doing this, and we had just as much fun as the kids who were given everything.

To be able to run fast was an essential survival skill for black kids in Memphis. If I saw a cop, my first reaction was always to run, and it did not matter if I had done anything wrong or not. The cops loved to chase kids, like we were part of a "Tom and Jerry" cartoon. One summer day several of my friends and I went into a hot dog joint called the Orange Bar. We had just ordered our hot dogs and sodas when four white policemen walked in. Without any provocation, the cops ordered us to line up against the wall. We knew the cops would search us, and one of my buddies had a knife in his pocket. He let it quietly slide onto the floor and gently pushed it with his toe to the next kid, who then pushed it on to his neighbor. When it got to me, I slid it over to Jason, who was the youngest of us and too frightened to notice what I had done. Poor Jason got caught. A policeman dragged him out of the lineup and threw him into the courtyard. Jason panicked when the four cops converged on him, and he began to babble his name, his father and mother's names, where they lived and worked, and a whole bunch of other irrelevant things. He was so frightened that he talked nonstop, covering his entire family history in the process. The rest of us kids could not control ourselves and we began laughing. Even the cops found it tremendously amusing.

There were so many restrictions put on blacks in those days. For example, we were not allowed to hang out on Main Street. When I tried to shine shoes on Main Street, the police ran me off and made me go back to Beale Street. If they caught me, they smashed my shoebox. No one could afford a shoeshine in our black neighborhood, so I would sneak back to Main Street, where I could make some money. I charged three cents for a regular shine and maybe a nickel for a spit shine, which meant I would spit on the customer's shoes to give them an extra layer of flow. I'd smack that shoe rag back and forth across their shoes and really make it sing. The louder that rag popped, the more money I made. But whenever the police showed up, I'd have to grab my shoebox and run.

We were allowed to shop on Main Street, but we could not eat anywhere or use a toilet. If you were a man, you used the alley. One day, when I was maybe twelve, I was peeing in the alley behind Main Street when the police stopped and looked down the alley. I had to stuff it quickly in my pants and get out of there. I was walking and peeing right down into my shoes. I laugh about this now, but if the police had caught me, they would have beat me up.

One day I walked into a grocery store and saw a fresh pound cake on the counter. When the clerk was not looking, I took the cake and hid it inside my coat. As I walked toward the door, the foil around the cake began to rustle. The lady screamed, "Stop thief!" and began to chase me. I ran several blocks before losing her by hiding in the drainage ditch under Neptune Street. By this time I had completely lost my appetite, so I broke the cake into small pieces, threw them into the water, and watched them float away. I was so embarrassed and frightened that I stayed hidden in that ditch until nightfall.

My mother was very religious. My stepfather would go to church, but his heart was not really in it. He liked to drink, smoke, chew tobacco, and gamble. He had only two black suits, which Mrs. Johnson had given him, and that's all he'd wear. Toosie did not like this. She wanted him to dress like the other men, who changed their suits when they went to church. Fred just did not care about clothes. He was a hardworking guy who did not care what he looked like. Toosie resented this. She'd tell him, "Why don't you buy some clothes?" As long as I knew him he had only those two black suits, but he always had money in his pocket.

Every Saturday night we took what we called our Sunday bath so we would be clean for Sunday school. Oh, yeah, we had to be spic-and-span for the Lord. We bathed in what we called a number three tub, which was simply a large tin tub. We'd heat the water on our kitchen stove and then we all shared the bathwater. My youngest sister, Kate, would take her bath; then I would take a bath in her bathwater. My mother would also fix my sisters' hair on Saturday night.

We went to Sunday school about 9:30, after which came the regular services. Momma used to give each of us a couple of pennies to put in the collection box in Sunday school, but I never put mine in. When the collection box came around, I'd tap it on the side, but I wouldn't drop anything in it. After Sunday school I'd take my pennies and go to the corner store and buy some candy. You could get a lot of candy for a couple of cents in those days. All the other kids would look at my candy and say, "Hey, gimme some." I'd tell them, "Get your own candy. You need to earn your own money and save your pennies just like I do." My sisters were so honest they would never do anything like this. We were not in the same Sunday school class, so they did not see what I was doing. Most of the time my sisters stayed for the 11 o'clock service, but I never did. I'd go to Sunday school, grab my two or three cents, and leave. Perhaps that's why my sisters turned out so well. Nellie now has her Ph.D., Alice is a retired schoolteacher, Barbara has her own business in Chicago, and Kate is a civil rights activist.

Things were cheap when I was growing up. You could go to a movie at the Daisy Theater for five cents if you arrived before six o'clock. When I helped my stepfather at Mrs. Johnson's, he'd pay me a dime. That meant I had to get to the theater before six o'clock or I would not have any money for candy. Fred would always make me work until the last minute, so I'd have to run as fast as I could the whole way. After a few times the ticket lady began to recognize me. I'd be running across the street yelling, "I'm coming; I'm coming." She would be changing the sign from five to ten cents, and I'd be yelling at her. She was so nice that she would not change the sign until I paid my nickel. They would sometimes show several different movies, and I'd stay until I had seen the last movie of the evening. Of course, blacks had to sit in a separate part of the theater, which usually was the balcony.

From the ages of five or six to maybe ten or eleven, black and white kids in the South occasionally played together. It was only when we were approaching our teens and puberty that we had to be kept separated. Whites had their reasons for this. When we were young, they thought of us in the same way they would a puppy or a kitten. We were cute, harmless little pets who existed for the amusement of their children. However, when we got older, and especially us boys, they considered us aggressive and dangerous.

As youngsters, we were not aware of just how sick all this was. Black and white kids just wanted to play football, baseball, marbles, or hide-and-seek on the vacant field that belonged to the Standard Oil Company. When we were young we often played together, but as we got older, they'd play at one end of the field and we'd play at the other end. Sometimes we had to fight the white kids to get a spot if they got there before we did. Or if they outnumbered us, they might chase us away.

There were few parks in Memphis for black people. Even if there was a park in a black neighborhood, it usually was considered a white park, and blacks were not allowed to walk through it. One such park was at South Parkway and Bellevue. The park is still there, and today blacks can go there and do whatever they want. But when I was a kid, blacks were not even allowed to step on the grass. We had to walk around the park to get where we were going. If we did not, whites would beat us up or the police would arrest us. Whites saw this as a violation of their system, and they could never allow that. Every time I passed that park, I wanted to play on the grass and the swings, but I knew exactly what would happen if I did.

 There were lots of parks for whites, but in all of Memphis the only three parks I remember for blacks were Lincoln Park, Henley Park, and one in Orange Mound. We had no golf courses. Golf was a white man's game that cost a lot of money, so it would not have made any difference whether we had a golf course or not.

Lincoln Park was located just off of Highway 51, and blacks would gather there for holidays and other festive occasions. Once a year, usually during election campaigns, some of the big companies in Memphis would throw a big picnic in Lincoln Park just for blacks. We'd get ribs for barbequing from the meatpacking companies and bread and beer from other distributors. At the end of the day, everyone would be full of food and very, very drunk.

We looked forward to this summer party. Thousands of blacks attended, but we paid a heavy price to get this free food and drink. No white people came, except politicians who wanted to give a speech during election time, and then they would have to have police protection. No way would any other whites come into that environment. It would be too dangerous for them. Blacks would sometimes fight among themselves, so you can imagine what might happen if a handful of whites started mixing with thousands of blacks. I went several times, but I was too young to pay much attention to what the politicians said. I was just there for the fun, swinging on the swings and sliding down the slides. Most blacks went for the free food and drink, not for anything else. Politics did not mean anything to blacks back then because we had no representatives in any elected office.

There were no integrated coffee or sandwich shops in Memphis. Whites would go to their own little restaurants and eat things like a bacon, tomato, and lettuce sandwich — a BTL they called it. I worked as a short order cook at the William Lucky Strike Bowling Alley for a few months while I was in high school, and I thought it would be wonderful if just once I could have a BTL sandwich. We also served toast with jelly, which I also thought sounded great. So every time the boss was not looking, I'd fix myself a BTL or a toast and jelly sandwich and run to the toilet and eat it. The boss did allow me one drink and one sandwich a day, but that wasn't enough for me. If he wasn't looking, I'd make one for the customer and one for me. I eventually ate so many sandwiches it became no big deal, and I got tired of them.

· · · · · ★ · · · · ·

I was always small for my age, but I was tough, and I liked the rough-and-tumble of street fighting. I was not that strong, but I was fast and very, very aggressive, and I would do anything to beat up the other guy. One day in eighth grade I stopped by our school gym and saw these guys training to box. I just stood there watching them. The coach asked me, "Hey, you look like you want to get in there with these boys."

I told him, "No, I don't."

He said, "Why don't you give it a try." I was hesitant because I had never really boxed before, and those kids knew all kinds of stuff. He insisted, "Come on, give it a try." So I got in the ring and they put the gloves on me. They had me go against the toughest guy in the gym. He was going to represent Porter School in the city's annual Golden Gloves tournament. I went right after him and hit him everywhere but on the bottom of his feet, and if he had raised them, I would have hit him there too. I used the same tactics in the ring that I had used every day in the streets. Of course, there are rules and regulations in the ring, so you cannot knee a guy or hit him below the belt.

The coach pulled me over and said, "You're pretty good, but we can make you better. How would you like to train with us?" Although I did not know much about boxing, he saw that I had what it took to win in the ring. I told the coach I would give it a try, and I did. I represented my school in the Golden Gloves tournament at the Beale Street Auditorium. Beale Street was the only street in Memphis that blacks could walk on and feel halfway free. The police would stop white people who tried to go down Beale Street. All the good things, and some things that were not so good, blacks could find on Beale Street, including the best blues music in America.

Blacks were, of course, only allowed to fight other blacks. In those days we would never be allowed to hit a white man, not even in a boxing competition. I also think some of those white boys did not want to fight us because we were so tough. That's why blacks have always been the best boxers, and not just in America but in the world.

The coach was black. At that time there were no whites coaching or doing anything else in black schools. Black teachers taught only black students, black doctors treated exclusively black patients, and black mailmen delivered mail only to blacks. It was total segregation. That's the kind of society I grew up in. It was shameful and unforgivable, especially when you consider we were all Americans.

My first boxing coach was paid nothing. He just came in when it was time to train for a tournament, like the Golden Gloves. After I graduated from the eighth grade and went into high school, I had another coach, and I continued to train. I was too small to play football or basketball, so boxing became my sport.

Our high school's athletic teams competed only against other black schools. Our football uniforms were hand-me-downs from a white school with the same colors. When the white players wore out their uniforms, they donated them to us. I remember we played against this black team from the small town of Marion, Arkansas. They did not even have uniforms as good as ours. Some of their players wore one football shoe and one tennis shoe. They did not have matching colors, and they knew nothing about football, but they were big and strong. We thought we were tough and well trained, but they just crushed us. Usually after we lost a game, we'd beat up the players on the other team, but we did not mess with those corn-fed Marion kids. They were too big and mean. But that was the only team we did not jump on.

Every black American who was alive during the 1930s remembers the second Joe Louis–Max Schmeling fight, when Louis knocked out the German on June 22, 1938. Schmeling had defeated Joe in their first fight and was considered the Great White Hope, especially in Germany, where he represented the Nazis and the so-called master race. The rumor in the black community was Schmeling had won the first fight because he had needles in his gloves, so every time he hit Joe, the blows would deaden his arm. We all wondered why the gloves had not been inspected before the fight. In the second fight, Joe knocked him out and broke two of his ribs, all in the first round. We sat around our radio and cheered like mad. It meant a lot to blacks to see the German superman defeated.

The last black heavyweight champion had been Jack Johnson, and whites were convinced that was an accident. Most whites in both Germany and America thought they belonged to the master race, but Joe Louis proved that there is no such thing as a master race. We were overjoyed, but we did not dare go out in the streets and celebrate openly. That was simply too dangerous in a racist country. We had to be careful in everything we did or risk retaliation.[5]

Blacks had to learn lots of things just to survive. I was a hustler, which meant I always knew where and how to make a buck, although sometimes conditions beyond my control would cost me my chance to make money. One summer, when I was maybe sixteen, I worked as a dishwasher at a small bar and grill, but I was fired because of the white girl who worked with me. She was from Chicago and was the boss's niece. She liked to talk to me, but blacks were not supposed to talk to white girls. Her uncle warned me, "You know, nigger, you're not allowed to talk to that white girl."

I washed the dishes in the back room, and she waited on the customers up front. But every chance she got, she came in the back and talked to me. I told her, "Don't talk to me." In fact, I begged her not to.

She'd say, "Well, in Chicago we don't mind talking to Negroes."

I'd tell her, "But this is not Chicago; this is Memphis, and you don't want to talk to me here." I knew the boss would fire me if he caught me talking to her again. Sure enough, he came in this one day and she was talking to me. So he called me into the back room and paid me off. I was making something like three dollars a week. He gave me my little envelope and told me to get the hell out of there. I was really angry with her because I had done nothing wrong. She had forced herself on me, and that cost me my job, but that's how it was in the South when I was growing up.

I did much better for myself when I worked at the Peabody Hotel, which was the most luxurious hotel in Memphis. It was a beautiful old hotel, and of course only white people could stay there. All of them were rich, and many owned cotton plantations. Another good hotel was the Claridge. The only way blacks could get inside hotels like these was to work there. We had to pay the headwaiter to work as porters, waiters, or room service boys. I would rush out of school, hop on a trolley, and then outrun the other black kids so I would be the first to pay the headwaiter my dollar bribe.

If I was lucky and got selected, I knew how to earn good tips. When a white man came in with his wife, I'd make a great show of respect toward her. The husband loved this because it made him feel important. I'd pull the chair out for her and seat her. I'd take their wraps, and if I saw any lint on their coats, I would brush it off with this little brush I always carried. I showed all this respect to make them think black folks really liked white folks and to build them up for the tip. Whether I sincerely liked them or not, well, that was a horse of another color. I just had to make them feel important, and they ate this up. Waiters do not usually do this today, but that was how we made our living.

In one night of working at the Peabody, I could make more money than my parents together made in an entire week. My mother made six or seven dollars a week at the White Rose Laundry, and my stepfather made maybe fifteen or sixteen dollars a week at the Memphis Furniture Factory. I could make up to twenty or thirty dollars in tips in a single night at the Peabody Hotel. Unfortunately, I did not get to work every night. There were so many of us competing for each night's work, and sometimes I'd get there a little too late.

When I worked room service, I kept small bottles of whisky in the basement locker where we put our school clothes and books. The white guests would call room service and order a drink. I made a lot of money serving them what we called after-hours whisky. I might pay $1.80 for a pint of whisky, but I'd sell it to them for five. It would be late at night, and they had nowhere else to get it. One night I really hit it lucky. This man called down for room service, and I took my whisky up to him. He was drunk and he mistakenly gave me a hundred dollar bill and said, "Here's a five, boy."

I looked at it and quickly said, "Thank you, sir. Thank you."

He said, "Keep the change."

"Thank you, sir. Thank you," and I quickly stuffed it in my pocket and immediately left the hotel. I was worried that when he sobered up he might come looking for me. In fact, I was so afraid he might remember me that I did not go back there to work for a long time. In those days that was a tremendous amount of money. The next day I went downtown and had me some big-legged pants made. We called them drapes, and only blacks wore drapes. I also bought a couple of nice shirts, some shoes, a light blue suit, and a pink overcoat. That made me really "clean," which meant well-dressed in Memphis black lingo.

Blacks liked pretty colors, and we certainly dressed differently than whites. Today, white boys wear the same kinds of clothes blacks do, but not when I was a boy. Back then white boys wore mostly khaki pants and plaid shirts, but no one could have made me dress like that.

· · · · · ★ · · · · ·

There were lots of blacks who made money because they knew how to hustle. Some were even able to send their kids to college. My stepfather was a good hustler. He always had money, but he also taught me not to be afraid of work. I did not agree with him on a lot of things, but I'm glad he taught me about working hard. There was no job that he would not do as long as he got paid for it. He was very smart for a man who had only three years of formal schooling. He had to leave Arkansas and come to Memphis because he and his brother beat up a white man. I never found out why they beat him up, but they both knew that once you jumped a white man, you had to flee.

That was the main reason I joined the army. As we used to say, "I had to book up," which meant I had to leave town. It happened one night when I was eighteen and several of us were hopping freight trains just for the fun of it. We'd wait at the K.C. Junction, where the trains slowed down to go north, south, east, or west. We'd hop a train going to Mississippi and then hop another one coming back. Sometimes we'd try to catch them when they were moving fast or perform crazy stunts just to prove our manhood. We would not just run up and hop on; we had to do it with style. We'd catch maybe the third rung from the bottom of the ladder, swing our feet out horizontally, and then swing them back and hook on. If your hands slipped, you could fall under the train, and that happened to a friend of mine. His hand slipped and the train cut off both legs. There he was. His body was lying on one side of the tracks and his legs on the other. He started laughing. I think he was hysterical, but we all started laughing: "Hey, man, that was cool." He survived and eventually got wooden legs, and he's still alive today.

This particular night five or six of us were waiting for a train when a white man came up and asked if we could find him a black woman. He looked like a hobo or a tramp. We all knew the situation, and we did not want any trouble. We understood if we did anything to him and the police caught us, we'd never get out of jail. We started to walk away from him, but he followed us and again asked, "Hey, boys, where can I get me a black woman?" We said to each other, "This guy must be crazy. Let's get out of here." My friend Nathan was bringing up the rear when all of a sudden he turned around and hit him. The white guy went down, and all of us stomped him. Then we left.

Earlier that same day I had been in a fight with a guy we called Bip Bop Bam, who was the neighborhood bully. He was a bad, bad dude and strong as a mule. Everyone was scared of Bip Bop Bam, and so was I. He was teasing my friend Jesse because he had a hole in his pants. Bip taunted him, "Every time I see you, I see your ragged ass." When I told Bip to leave Jesse alone, he walked up and hit me in the head. I went down, and he jumped on top of me and banged my head against the sidewalk. I could see stars and was about to lose consciousness. Everyone was standing around looking and laughing. But I had a small knife in my pocket, which we all carried. We called them frog-stickers. I did not enjoy cutting anybody, but he was beating the devil out of me and I thought he might kill me. So I pulled my knife out and popped open the blade with one hand, which was something we all practiced. I reached up and grabbed him by the collar and pulled him down toward me. I choked the knife, which means I held it so it could go in only so deep and not kill him. I got my hand between his chest and my body and started stabbing him in the chest. He began to scream, "Let me up! Let me up!" The other guys were still laughing because they could not see what I was doing. When I turned him loose, he jumped up and ran away. I got up, dusted myself off, and went home.

Bip went to John Gaston Hospital, where they bandaged him up because he was bleeding so badly. Later, one of the guys came to my house and told me that Bip was looking for me. I was worried. I knew he liked to sneak up behind someone and hit him in the head with a baseball bat. I was really afraid of him, and I did not want him to find me. All this had happened earlier the same day we beat up the white guy by the train tracks.

The next morning I was eating breakfast and getting ready to go to school when there was a loud knock on our screen door. It was the police, and they were looking into the house through the ragged screen. They could see straight through the house into the kitchen, but fortunately I was sitting at the end of the kitchen table where they could not see me. My mother went to the door, and I heard the police ask, "Is Skippy home?" I still have no idea how they knew my nickname. In such a situation, every black American knows to tell the police nothing, and especially not where somebody is. My mother said, "No, he's not here. What do you want with him?" The police refused to tell her. I could hear all this from the kitchen, so I peeked around the corner, and I could see these two monstrous white policemen pounding their hands with their billy clubs. I figured they were going to whomp me good, but I was also wondering why they were looking for me. Was it for beating up the white man or for knifing Bip? I had enough sense not to stick around and find out.

I ran out the back door and down the railroad track and kept right on running until I got downtown to Front Street, where there was an army recruiting station. Right then and there, on September 11, 1947, I joined the army. I had no idea for which crime the police wanted me. I just knew I could not wait around to find out.

They tested me at the recruiting station, and I scored high enough that I could have gone in the air force, but I chose the army. This was early morning, and there was a troop train leaving that very afternoon for Biloxi, Mississippi, where I would take my physical exam and be inducted into the service. The recruiting sergeant told me I could leave the building but to be back by 1:30, but I stayed right there. When he noticed that I was still hanging around, he asked, "Hey, are you still here?" I told him I did not have anywhere to go. Actually, I did not want to leave because I was afraid the police might find me, and I knew they would never think to look for me at the recruiting station. If they were really after me, they would be scouring the black neighborhoods.

I was real nervous until I boarded that train that afternoon. When it finally pulled out of the station, I heaved a great sigh of relief because I knew I had escaped the police. I had not even called home, so nobody knew where I was. Only later did I write my mother and tell her that her only son had become a soldier.

CHAPTER TWO

U.S. Army Combat Soldier: Korea

In spite of the resistance of military and political leaders, African Americans have willingly, and often heroically, fought and died in every American military conflict, going back as far as the eighteenth-century skirmishes and wars against the Indians, the French, and of course the British. Unfortunately, two hundred years of military duty and sacrifice did not free black soldiers from second-class status. Even during America's World War II fight against Hitler's Third Reich and its heinous racial policies, the U.S. Army continued to segregate its troops, and even its blood banks. In 1948 President Harry S. Truman took an important first step when he ordered an end to a segregated military, but Clarence Adams and all other African American soldiers were still serving in segregated units when the Korean War broke out in June 1950.

The train from Memphis took me and the other recruits to Biloxi, Mississippi, where I was officially sworn in to the army. Biloxi was a totally segregated city. White soldiers were allowed to go into town in the evening, but not us. Our sergeants told us it was not safe for blacks to leave the camp. So we spent one week totally restricted. I was, however, given a choice for basic training: I could go to a Northern camp or remain in the South. I had heard that blacks had more freedom in the North, so that's where I chose to go.

Three of my uncles had fought in World War II, and when they came home in 1945, they told me lots of stories about Europe. Their experiences and enthusiasm about defeating the Nazis made a deep impression on me. My uncle King Adams, who was only a few years older than I, had talked about places in this world where there was no racial discrimination. In unmistakable language he told

Some people accuse me of being bitter, but I was forced to be. It certainly wasn't my idea.
—Clarence Adams

We black soldiers soon realized the bitter irony of our situation—supposedly fighting to protect the freedom of American society, even as that freedom was denied us in our own country.
—Curtis James Morrow, What's a Commie Ever Done to Black People: A Korean War Memoir

me, "You can't even look at a white woman here in Memphis, but you can fuck one in Europe." He also said, "In a northern city like Chicago, blacks can even eat with whites in the same restaurant." His words really impressed me, but unfortunately, I discovered that in many ways the North was even worse than the South.

I was stationed for three months at Fort Dix, just outside Trenton, New Jersey, and I hated every minute of it. I did, however, learn a very important lesson: No matter where you are or what people say, you suffer discrimination if you are black. In fact, some of the worst racists are in the North, and especially in Boston. Hell, I don't even like blacks from Boston. I beat up this black guy in the army who called himself a Bostonian. He was typical of those Northern blacks who look down on their Southern brothers. When he said to me, "I am a Bostonian," I told him, "Well, I'm a Memphian," and I proceeded to whomp the devil out of him.

I have to admit, I could be very nasty back then. At five-foot-six inches and 126 pounds, I was the smallest guy in my squad, so I wanted to be the meanest. The same thing was true in the prisoner of war camps. If I was going to survive, I had to be tougher than anybody else, but there were also times when my toughness was of little help, and these situations often involved racism.

I learned the hard way that bigotry in the North was different than in the South. When our train arrived in Trenton, a military bus was waiting to take us to camp, where we were supposed to eat breakfast, but I decided I was not going to take that bus. They had given us meal tickets on the way up, and I had sold some of mine, which meant I had money in my pocket. I figured I could take a taxi later. There I was, an American soldier all dressed up in my spanking new uniform, ready to defend my country, and determined to eat breakfast in this supposedly free and equal North.

I started looking for this restaurant of my dreams, and not far from the train station I found it. There was no "Whites Only" sign hanging in the window, so I went in and took a seat. Two white waitresses were leaning on the counter talking to each other. I sat there, expecting one of them to wait on me. They looked over at me but kept right on talking. I began to wonder what was going on. I glanced around the restaurant and saw that the only people there were a bunch of old white men drinking coffee and reading the morning paper. I noticed that they were peeking over their newspapers at me, obviously wondering what I was doing in their restaurant. I began to get real nervous. I simply did not know how to act in the North. I took a half-dollar out of my pocket and tapped it on the table. The waitresses again looked at me but went

Army recruit Clarence Adams

right on talking. Finally, a white man came in, took a seat, and immediately received service.

I began to tremble because I had never before faced anything like this. In the South I always knew where I was not allowed, but in the North there were no "Whites Only" signs. This was even more degrading, and what made it even worse, I did not know how to handle the situation.

I knew I had to leave, but the walk from that table to the exit was the loneliest I have ever taken. I thought I would never reach that door. Nobody said a word. Clearly, those people enjoyed seeing me hurting. It was as if I did not even exist. Because of my lofty expectations for the North, this was a painful and humiliating experience, and the anger has stayed with me.

This incident also made me realize there was no difference between North and South, except that Northerners were shrewder and more hypocritical, whereas Southerners let you know precisely how they felt. From then on, I never liked the North, and I still do not. Years later Malcolm X put it best: "The Mason-Dixon line begins at the Canadian border."

In spite of the racism, I still wanted to get off base. When I got a weekend pass, I went to Philadelphia or New York, but never back to Trenton. Two or three of us would pool our money, get a hotel room, go to the bars, and try to have a good time. Harlem was the best place to go, especially if we ran out of money. We could go to the Harlem USO Club, and they'd give us some coffee and donuts and find a way to get us back to camp.

· · · · · ★ · · · · ·

I finished my basic and advanced training as a machine gunner in the infantry in December 1947 and immediately shipped out for my first tour of duty in Korea. I was in the 159th Military Patrol in Korea for almost a year, until the Americans and the Russians agreed to pull most of their troops out of Korea in 1948.

Unfortunately, I messed up a few times in Korea. The first time was during my initial tour in Korea when I fell asleep on guard duty. The second time was also during my first Korean tour when the army put me in a firefighter unit and a sergeant assigned me to drive a fire truck. The problem was, I did not know how to drive. Nevertheless, when he ordered me to back the truck into the garage, I did—right through the back wall. When I was hauled before the colonel, I told him I was just obeying orders and that the sergeant had never asked me if I could drive, but I was still court-martialed.

I also got in trouble during my second tour in Korea, which was actually during the war. I went into the city of Inchon, got drunk, and did not return to camp when I was supposed to. I had some money, so I just stayed in town and partied. I drank a lot of unrefined rice wine, which is called makkolli, and ate platefuls of kimchi, which is hot, spicy, fermented cabbage. Oh, yeah, I associated with the local people and had lots of fun. I even learned to sing Korean songs. Everywhere I've gone, I've learned from the people.

Some of my unit officers were convinced I was trying to get out of the army. They sent me to a military psychiatrist to determine if I was crazy enough to be discharged. The main thing he asked me was why I joined the army. I told him, "Hey, I joined the army to fight for my country." I just played with him and gave him all the right answers.

Finally he said, "Well, there's nothing wrong with you."

I told him, "I know. That's why I'm in the army." So he sent me back to my unit.

After I finished my first tour of duty in Korea in December of 1948, I was sent to Japan, where I was stationed in Gifu in the 25th Division, 24th Infantry Regiment. Japan was a bad experience for many black soldiers. The army stationed blacks basically in two places: Yokohama and Gifu. Osaka, Tokyo, and several other cities were for white soldiers. We were not even supposed to set foot in Tokyo. If the white military police found us in the city, they went after us. I knew all about this, so I never went to Tokyo. I did not want to put myself in a position that would get me in more trouble for not behaving the way the military demanded.

Many of the Japanese people also did not like blacks because white soldiers had told them all kinds of stories, including that black soldiers had tails like monkeys. But this was not true in Gifu and Yokohama. In those cities the Japanese women clearly preferred the "chocolate soldiers" over the "milk soldiers." Of course, we told them bad things about white soldiers just as the whites did about us. I knew that the same thing had happened in Europe after the Second World War. White soldiers told German and French women that blacks had monkey tails, but those women wanted to see for themselves. So the blacks told them, "You want to see my tail? Let me show you. Hey, I'm wearing it backwards."

I must admit that many American soldiers, including blacks, left babies behind in Japan, but this was seldom because of rape. The mothers were usually prostitutes who got pregnant. The guys then shipped out, leaving their babies behind. There were thousands of these babies, both white and black, and it was certainly nothing to be proud of.

I did have a Japanese girlfriend. Her parents were peasant farmers who had very little money. I don't know that she really loved me, but she knew I could provide her with comforts her parents could not. My army pay was not much, but I was a very good gambler and won lots of money playing poker and shooting craps. In fact, I won so much money, I sent half my army pay home and put most of the rest in savings in the U.S. Army's Soldiers Deposit Program. I lived off my gambling winnings and still had enough to buy this girl a house, which I gave her when I left Japan. Before I left, her family gave me a beautiful antique tea set, made from the finest porcelain. I sent it home to my mother, and we still have it.

For the most part we had very little contact with Japanese families, other than perhaps seeing them in the teahouses, where we'd drink tea or sake and maybe eat some rice or shrimp. I did something once in a teahouse that really embarrassed me, and I vowed never do it again. I was talking with a Japanese businessman who asked me how life in America was for a black man. I did not want him to look down on me so I told him, "We all live alike in America, white or black."

He let me talk on and on like this, until he finally said, "You know, I've spent quite a bit of time in America."

I could have dropped through the floor. He knew that life was not the same for blacks and whites in the States, but he had let me go on and on telling him how well blacks lived. I was so embarrassed that I vowed never again to lie about the race situation in America, and I never have.

I saw American soldiers do many stupid things to the Japanese people. I was pulling guard duty on the docks in Kobe, and my partner was a little black guy who was even smaller than I. In fact, he was about the smallest thing I ever saw in the army. I did not know his real name, but we called him Aggie John. We were on Pier One when along comes this old Japanese man. He was at least sixty years old and not doing anything to anybody. Aggie decided he wanted to beat him up, so he walked over and hit him in the stomach. The old man doubled over, and Aggie looked back at me and said, "See how hard I can hit."

I yelled at him, "What in the hell are you doing?" He mumbled something about "slant-eyed Japanese," and he hit him again. I told him, "Hey, stop that! Would you want somebody to do you like that?" I was thinking of what happened so often to blacks back home. "That's the way we've been treated. If you do that again, I'll kill you." I threw a round in my carbine and told him, "Aggie, I'm not playing. If you do that again, I'm going to shoot you."

He said, "You mean you'd kill me over this old Japanese guy?"

I said, "Yes, because he's never done anything to you." Aggie got real angry and went back to the barracks and told the guys, "Hey, Adams stuck up for a Jap." But when I told the guys what had happened, they all sided with me.

What goes around, comes around. The same thing happened to me when I was a prisoner in Korea. Some young boys began pushing me around, and an old man saved my life. Just maybe, because I had saved that old man in Japan, somebody did something similar for me. Life is funny that way. I know after I went to China, this positive attitude helped me establish good relations with the common people.

· · · · · ★ · · · · ·

My most enjoyable times in Japan occurred when I boxed on the post team. Boxing granted me special privileges, and most of my time was spent training, fighting, and partying after my fights. I really loved boxing. I had begun fighting while I was in junior high school in Memphis, so I had lots of experience even before I joined the service. Several guys from Memphis would bet on me because I was winning all my fights. Even the officers bet on me. I liked that, so I would fight even harder. This one lieutenant wanted to bet on me against a much larger opponent. He told me, "Hey, I'll take care of you if you beat him." So I beat him; I beat him bad. I did not knock him out, but I dominated him for three rounds, which was as long as our bouts lasted.

When a fight only lasts three rounds, you have to fight hard the entire time because you have so little time to prove yourself. You simply have to destroy your opponent quickly. From the opening bell I would leap across the ring and do as much damage as I could. I'd really jump on a guy. Because I was so quick, I could hit most of the guys faster than they could hit me. If my opponent hit me once, I'd hit him four or five times. My left hook earned me the nickname "Greased Lightning" because someone said I was so fast you could put oil on my moves. I feared no one, and I never lost a match.

I started out as a featherweight at 126 pounds, but I gained weight and eventually fought at 140 pounds. I had enough confidence in myself that I also fought above my weight class. I would fight anybody. My hardest fight was during my first tour in Korea. I fought a South Korean soldier, and he almost beat me. No matter how hard I hit him, it did not faze him, but every time he hit me, I felt it. The judges finally gave the fight to me, but whether I really won it or not, I don't know. My ribs were sore, and I was hurting for days.

After my tour in Japan, I was shipped back to Fort Lewis, Washington, to be discharged. This was the summer of 1950, and I only had a short time left on my enlistment. In fact, I had already begun processing my discharge papers.

Then on June 25, 1950, we heard over the PA system that President Truman had announced the outbreak of the Korean War and had ordered all soldiers with less than a year on their enlistment to be extended for twelve months.

I was very upset because I was looking forward to getting out of the army and making a living as a professional boxer. A promoter in San Francisco who had a small stable of fighters had offered to help me start my professional career. All I had to do was prove myself. I figured this was my only chance. I did not have a high school diploma or any career skills, and what I had learned in the army was not going to help me in civilian life. So what was I going to do? I was a strong young man, but like so many poor, uneducated youngsters, all I knew how to do was fight. Now, because of the war, I had lost that opportunity. The only time I boxed again was as a POW, although when I was in China, sports officials talked about putting together an Olympic boxing team. Unfortunately, some higher-ranking officials canceled the idea because they insisted boxing was too barbaric.

My final act before boarding the ship for my second tour in Korea was to call home. I told my mother, "Momma, I'm going to Korea to fight the North Koreans, but don't be concerned about me. If I should come up missing, don't worry. I'll be alive somewhere. If so much as one guy lives, that'll be me." I didn't hear her voice or see her again for sixteen years.

We sailed directly from Fort Lewis, Washington, to Pusan, Korea. By the time we arrived in August of 1950, the North Koreans had trapped our troops in the Pusan perimeter in the southeastern corner of Korea and were threatening to push them back into the Sea of Japan. When we landed at Pusan, all we saw was total confusion. There were tents and equipment scattered all over the landscape and people running in every direction, but because the situation was so desperate along the Naktong River, we spent only one day in Pusan before being ordered to the front.

Before I was sent over, I had been trained as an infantry machine gunner, but because of heavy casualties, I was now put in the artillery, although I knew nothing about big guns. In fact, I had never touched an artillery piece, but that's how the military works. I was assigned to Battery A of the 503rd Field Artillery, an all-black regiment in the 2nd Division. I became an ammo bearer in a 120-man battery that had six 155 mm howitzers. It was my second day in Korea, I knew no one, I was in a strange outfit, and I was right smack in the middle of a shooting war.

I had no idea what I was doing, but I was all excited. I thought, hey, bring on that big bad enemy. I'll treat him just like I treated all those guys in the boxing ring. I could not wait to see him, but when I did, and he started shooting, I was no longer so anxious to see him.

When we first reached the front lines, things seemed to be going all right, but then we bogged down. We suffered heavy casualties, and I began to realize that war is not a game, and I could get hurt. With bullets now flying in both directions, I began thinking about my own survival.

We had been told that ours was a well-equipped army, and that the North Koreans were nothing but a few ill-equipped, ragtag soldiers fighting with World War II Japanese rifles. I figured that with all our modern equipment, destroying them would be no problem; but I soon found out it was not going to be that easy. They fought fiercely, and I gained respect for them. Nevertheless, we eventually defeated them along the Naktong and pushed them northward out of the Pusan perimeter, but we lost many, many soldiers.

We gradually fought our way north, but small groups of enemy soldiers constantly emerged from nowhere and attacked us on our flanks or from the rear. These surprise attacks were unnerving, and I would often see guys praying. The battle would be raging, but somehow these guys found time to pray. I was always too busy firing my rifle during a firefight to worry about praying. I would not have prayed anyway, but a lot of guys did, and for some of them it was the first time. I thought, now that they are scared and in trouble, they're praying. They were trying to fool the Lord, so I figured He would surely get them shot.

One of these religious guys tried to convince me about the value of prayer. We were sitting together on the side of a small hill when all of a sudden mortars started raining down on us. One nearby soldier was blown to bits. There was no cover, so we were totally exposed. The guy crouched down next to me looked at me and asked, "Don't you pray?"

I turned to him and said, "I haven't prayed up to this point, so why should I start now? Besides, the Almighty knows how rotten I've . . ." I never finished my sentence. I heard a slight popping sound, as if someone had just opened a wine bottle. I looked over and saw that he had quietly fallen on his side. A sniper's bullet had ripped through his skull. I did not even know his name. Because I had transferred into this unit my second day in Korea, I never knew any of these guys. I did not ask anybody his name, and nobody ever bothered to find out who I was.

Ours was an all-black regiment, except for some of the officers. The army had first begun integrating white and black soldiers after the Chinese crossed the Yalu River in November of 1950 and almost wiped us out. We had so few men left they had to use white and black soldiers together to keep up the fight. When I was captured, the prisoners with me, black and white, did not even know the army had mixed some of its units. It was later in the prison camp that newly captured prisoners told us the army had done this. They had to scrape up everyone they could just to make up a unit. That's also when the white commanders found out blacks could fight.[1]

The white officers in my unit did not associate with us except to give us orders. We had one officer who was black, but only one. From the NCOs down, everybody was black. There was a white officer, whose name I don't remember, who was sitting next to me on a hillside during a lull in the fighting. He told me he was from Memphis, but that was the end of the conversation.

Initially, I believed we were there to help the Korean people, that we were freeing them from the North Korean Communists so they could enjoy the fruits of democracy. But it did not take me long to become disillusioned, especially about the role of the black soldier in Korea.

I could not understand how white America expected us to fight hard overseas when we were treated so badly at home. How could we really believe we were fighting for our country? To be honest, once we were put on the front lines, we fought to survive. We did not feel any lofty mission. When the battle came to us, we had no choice but to fight in order to live. You fight hardest when it's something you truly believe in, but what were we fighting for? To be oppressed? To be segregated? So the whites could continue their discrimination against us after we returned home?

A lot of us had relatives who had served during the Second World War. They told us they had fought, and some had died, for the United States because they were convinced that when they returned home, things would be better. But nothing changed, and they were still second-class citizens. Particularly in the South, whites lost no opportunity to remind these veterans that they were still black. In Europe many of them had mixed with whites, but this was still America, and in the South there would be no equality.

So there we were, five years later, on the front lines in another war, facing the same kinds of discrimination the older members of our families had faced during and after World War II. Some of us also began to understand that the North Koreans had not done anything to us, so why were we there trying to kill each other?

I had to try and push these negative thoughts out of my mind and continue to fight well and hard to survive, but I became increasingly determined not to jeopardize my chances of making it out of Korea alive. Early on I had noticed that during lulls on the battlefields some of the white boys wanted to kill so badly they'd shoot chickens, pigs, and other animals. They simply wanted to kill something. But blacks did not do things like that. When we got a chance to rest, we rested. I no longer felt any excitement about killing. When I first went into battle, I wanted to match my skills against the enemy, to see if I was tougher than he was, but not anymore.

As we moved farther north, we saw more and more civilian refugees. They were dragging along all their belongings, and many women had babies on their backs. I frequently saw young kids and old women lying dead alongside the roads. Sometimes tanks would just run over them. More and more I asked myself, What kind of war is this where such things happen? Should we really be here killing innocent civilians?

People back home later accused us of having been brainwashed by the Chinese, but even before Mao's troops entered the war, some of us had begun to think that the war was stupid and increasingly questioned the role we were supposed to play. For black soldiers this was sort of a hush-hush thing we whispered about among ourselves. If we talked openly, the military could have accused us of being cowards in the face of the enemy and had us court-martialed. After all, we had raised our right hand and sworn to fight for our country. But among ourselves we said, "What do we want with Korea? Korea can't hurt us. The Koreans can't fly to America and do anything to us." We had begun to talk like this, but very, very quietly.[2]

After General MacArthur ordered the Inchon landing on September 15, 1950, effectively cutting off the North Koreans' supply lines, my regiment advanced rapidly northward. We still had to fight, and during one of these skirmishes I moved from ammo bearer to gunner. Our gunner was killed, and the captain, who perhaps knew my math and aptitude scores from my army records, made me a gunner right then and there. I was put on what we called our base gun, which meant we'd fire one shot for accuracy, and if our shell landed in the right area, the other guns would be given the same coordinates and ordered to shoot. I had to learn how to calculate elevation, deflection, charge, and other factors. It was not simple, but I always had a good memory. Once you showed me how to do something, I could do it.

We eventually routed the North Korean Army and pushed them back over the Thirty-eighth Parallel. Our original goal was to liberate South Korea, after which many of us thought we should stop, but MacArthur ordered us to push on. He and his command staff insisted there were only a few pockets of North Korean resistance left, and these would soon be eliminated. This was the beginning of November 1950, and MacArthur promised we would be home for Christmas, just as soon as we wiped out those few remaining North Korean soldiers.

Our 2nd Division pushed steadily north to Pyongyang, which was the capital of North Korea. We rested there for a few days and regrouped before moving on to Kunu-ri, some fifty miles to the north. By this time my battery had become part of a regimental combat team. I will never forget how bitterly cold it was. The winter of 1950 came early and was the coldest in over twenty years. By late November the hills were covered with two feet of snow. It was so cold you could spit and it would freeze before it hit the ground. Many of us had only our summer uniforms, and our ammunition was running low. At the time, this did not really bother us because we knew we would soon be heading home.

I enjoyed my last warm meal in Kunu-ri. It was Thanksgiving dinner, with all the trimmings. We had fresh turkey, cranberry sauce, and beer that had been flown in from the States. Some regiments reportedly even had white tablecloths and candlelight, although we certainly did not. It would be three long years before I got another decent meal. Of course, for a lot of my buddies, that Thanksgiving dinner was their last supper.

Ignoring repeated warnings from the Chinese that they would enter the war if we kept advancing toward their border, MacArthur's troops pushed on to the Yalu River, which separated the Korean peninsula from mainland China. In the meantime, beginning already in October, the Chinese had been secretly sending in thousands of soldiers. They would hide and rest during the day and move only at night. By the time I was sitting down for my second plate of Thanksgiving turkey, some 260,000 Chinese soldiers were already dug in on the nearby hills.

On November 25, the day after Thanksgiving, Mao sprang his trap with an all-out attack from every direction. Chinese troops were everywhere — on the mountaintops, the hillsides, in the valleys — and thousands of American troops were trapped. At first we did not know they were Chinese, because our military leaders were still telling us the Chinese would not dare enter the war. Even after some of our soldiers reported fighting against Chinese soldiers, these same military commanders continued to insist that there were only North Koreans out there.

My regiment was hit hard and slowly tried to pull back. For the next several days we got no sleep. We did not even have time to eat, because we were frantically trying to stop the Chinese from overrunning us. We'd set up our big guns, fire them, load them on the big tractors that carried them, and move on to the next rice paddy, where we'd do the same thing again. The Chinese were all around us, constantly firing at us, and we knew it was just a matter of time before they got us. At dawn on November 29, I noticed that the 105 mm light artillery regiment was in full retreat. I immediately asked, "Where are those white boys going?" No one answered. In the afternoon a company of white infantrymen also retreated past us, and we were ordered to turn our 155 mm guns around and lay down cover fire so these white troops could escape. At that point I realized something was terribly wrong. According to conventional military strategy, heavy guns, such as those my regiment had, always had to be protected by infantry and light artillery, but now just the opposite was happening. As a result, when it came time for us to go, we had nobody to protect us. We did have some light weapons, but we were not set up to fight like an infantry unit. There was little doubt in my mind that our black regiment was being sacrificed to save white troops.

Without support, our heavy artillery pieces and the cumbersome tractors that transported them were sitting ducks for enemy mortar fire and machine guns. We kept firing, but by the end of the day we had run out of shells for our big guns. Our only chance was to wait for darkness and try to drive our tractors down this narrow road out of the valley where we were trapped.

I was riding on the top of the second tractor firing the mounted 50-caliber machine gun at the enemy troops in the surrounding hills. Suddenly the road narrowed down to almost nothing, and our column came to an abrupt halt. Mortar rounds, grenades, and machine gun fire poured down on us from all directions. Our lead vehicle was immediately disabled. The Chinese then knocked out the rear tractor. We were trapped. I jumped off my tractor, grabbed a 30-caliber machine gun, which was the weapon I had operated when I was an infantryman, and slid underneath the tractor and began firing. When my machine gun drew too much attention, I picked up a carbine and moved on to another tractor.

By now it was dark, but you could still see because everything was on fire. A Chinese machine gunner hiding behind the roadblock in front of us had us pinned down. We had to knock him out if we had any hope of escaping. A corporal named Eddie grabbed several hand grenades and moved out to get him. I told him he could not make it because he had too much ground to cover, but he said, "I can get him. I can get him." He crawled about ten yards and threw his grenades. When the machine gun ceased firing, Eddie jumped up and ran forward to see if he had killed him. He had not, and he was cut in half by a barrage of bullets.

That was enough for me. I knew I had to get out of there. There was a rice paddy alongside us, and on the other side of it I could see a mountain pass that was now the only way out. The problem was how to get across the rice paddy. I had no idea how many of us were left; in fact, not until I was a POW in Camp 5 did I find out that only nine or ten of the 120 men in my battery had survived.

I watched small bunches of our guys jump up and try to run across that open rice paddy, but every time a group tried this, they got mowed down by Chinese machine guns. I decided I would be better off going on my own. I let the next group of four or five jump up and dash across the paddy and then waited about ten seconds before taking off by myself in a slightly different direction. The machine gunners concentrated on the big group and did not shoot at me. I just kept running and never looked back.

It was a moonless night, and I had no way of knowing which way to go. I ran as fast as I could toward what I thought was south. At a bend in this mountain path, I almost collided with another fellow who was running in the opposite direction. Against the white snow, this shadowy figure looked like an enemy soldier. Before I could pull up my gun, the shadow fired. It was a Russian-made burp gun. I had learned to fear its distinct sound on the battle-fields. He missed, and the bullets whizzed over my head. I emptied my carbine in his direction, but I also missed. There was no time to change the magazine, so I turned around and ran as fast as I could. After a bit, I glanced back. The enemy soldier was not running after me; he was running away, just like I was! I thought to myself, "That son of a bitch is just as scared as I am."

I ran aimlessly that entire night. A couple of times I heard Oriental voices that could have been South Korean, but I could not take a chance. It was at least twenty degrees below zero, and my leather combat boots were filled with snow. Finally, I dropped from exhaustion and passed out. When I woke up in the snow the next morning, my entire body felt frozen, but especially my feet.

I knew there was no chance for a black man to walk through those snow-covered hills infested with thousands of enemy soldiers. I spotted a bunch of dead GIs and crawled over and lay down among them. I planned to play dead until nightfall. Suddenly I heard English-speaking voices. A dozen or so Americans, both white and black, along with a couple of British soldiers and a Turk were passing by. I was overjoyed to see them. None of us knew where we were or which direction was south. We made our best guess, which turned out to be wrong. We had walked for about an hour when the last person in line whispered, "We're being followed." We set up an ambush at a turn in the path, but no one walked into it. One of our guys said, "We must be walking in the wrong direction; otherwise they would have attacked us." We decided to turn around, but it was too late. The first barrage of gunfire killed six or seven of our guys.

Sergeant Richards, who was a black guy from Texas, and I took off together. We ran until we jumped into a shallow ditch. All of a sudden this Chinese soldier and his gun were staring down at us. We still had our guns, but we knew it was all over. I was afraid, but I still did not want to give up. Sergeant Richards was a tech sergeant and I was just a buck sergeant, so he outranked me. He said, "Look, I've got five children. I'm going to take my chances with him." I told him that was okay with me. Richards threw out his rifle and his .45 pistol. I pulled the clip out of my carbine and stuck it down in my belt. I then threw out the empty gun. My thinking was, I'm giving him my weapon, but I'm not going to let him kill me with my own bullets. If he's going to kill me, he's going to have to use his bullets. By this time I was thinking a whole lot of crazy things.

When he saw my empty gun, he went crazy. He started kicking and stomping the weapon. He obviously wanted to know where the bullets were. We could not talk to each other, but I knew what he wanted, so I pulled out my clip and threw it to him. After that he was all right.

We were lucky we threw out our guns instead of trying to shoot him. After we climbed out of the ditch, we looked around, and standing there were four more Chinese soldiers. I was that close to dying! They could just as easily have shot us. Then this Chinese soldier came up and hugged me. What a shock! Then he hugged Richards and motioned for us to sit down. He took his grain pack from around his neck and poured each of us a handful of grain. We had been fighting and running for several days without eating. I think he knew our situation, so he gave us some of his own food. We could not believe it. I ate my handful real quick, but when I put my hand out for more, he got angry and cursed me out. I did not understand the words, but I am sure he was telling me I was too damn greedy. I told him, "Hey, that's okay. I don't want anymore." [3]

I was captured on November 30, 1950. I was listed as missing for a year, until the Chinese released a list of prisoners to the Americans. My family had given me up for dead. They had no idea I was in a prisoner of war camp. The military had a $10,000 death benefit on each of us, and they paid Momma this money. Fortunately, she put it in the bank rather than spending it. When the military discovered I was still alive, they demanded the return of this money.

That was terrible because Momma had been suffering for a year thinking I was gone, but at least she had the money.

I hate to say this, but I discovered only after I finally returned home in 1966 that my being still alive somehow had made Momma kind of mad at me. I guess she thought, "What are you doing still alive?" I now can laugh about her being upset because she was going to lose that money, but at the time the thought did enter my mind that maybe I should have said, "Hey, I'm sorry that I'm still here." Maybe that's why she hates me so much, having to give up all that money. At that time, $10,000 was a whole lot of money.

CHAPTER THREE

Captured!

A soldier *suffers a series of shocks during and immediately after being captured. One moment he is ostensibly an independent entity fighting for his country. The next he is reduced to a helpless object at the mercy of his enemies. Often hungry and sleepless, sometimes wounded and feeling an element of shame about the capture itself, and certainly fearing possible execution, the new prisoner faces a most uncertain future. And for Clarence Adams, who believed that he and his fellow African American soldiers had been needlessly sacrificed by their white officers, there was also a deep-seated anger.*

More than 50 per cent of the Americans captured in 1950 did not survive captivity.[1] These men were victimized by long, deadly marches, under conditions so horrific that many of those already weakened by exhaustion, wounds, bad drinking water, and bitterly cold weather never made it to the permanent camps located along the Yalu River. Often, when a man could no longer march and fell by the wayside, he was shot. Even among those who made it to the camps, thousands were in such poor shape that they did not survive their first winter.

Because of frostbitten feet and an infected right leg, Clarence Adams was one of those who dropped out of the march following his capture on November 30, 1950. Miraculously, he was not shot when he no longer could keep up; in fact, as he suggests in his narrative, this might well have been one of the few times when it helped to be black. Later, as he struggled alone and near death on an isolated mountain footpath, an old Korean man mysteriously appeared to save him from some young toughs who probably meant to kill him. Such is the serendipity that often plays a decisive role in wartime; but it was not simply luck that allowed Adams to survive. Above all, it was his great personal courage and unyielding determination to live that proved decisive when a lesser person would simply have given up.

"You are not the exploiters! You are the exploited!"
— Chinese soldier who captured Clarence Adams

Shortly after we were captured, a frontline Chinese interpreter came up to Sergeant Richards and me, and I will never forget his words: "You are not the exploiters!" Then he paused. "You are the exploited!" I had no idea what he meant. Is that what I am, I thought, the exploited? He explained, "When you pick up a gun, you are our enemy. When you lay down your gun, you are our friend." He smiled and hugged Richards and me. I smiled back and thought to myself, So glad to be your friend. I guess that means you won't shoot me right away. At that moment, I certainly did not mind being the exploited if I could be his friend. Then he said, "I have to go now and welcome the others." Richards and I looked at each other in bewilderment.

A Chinese mortar squad had captured us, and they made us carry their Russian-made 120 mortar. They gave Richards the tube, which is lighter, and strapped the steel base to my back, even though I was much smaller than Richards. I had to carry that base up and down those mountains, and Richards knew I was tired. He tried to indicate that he and I should switch loads, but they would not hear of it. They kept pointing at me and signaling that I had to carry the base. The longer I walked, the heavier it got. When we sat down to rest, Richards would have to pull me up because I could not get up by myself. After a few hours, the mortar squad left us, but only after assigning a guard to take us to what we later discovered was a central gathering place for prisoners.

At one point I thought the guard was going to kill both of us. We were coming down the side of a mountain, and several F-86 jets strafed, napalmed, and killed a bunch of Chinese soldiers who had been walking through the valley. That did not bother me so much, but what really sickened me was when one of their napalm bombs hit a Korean hut. A woman with a baby on her back came running out of the house, engulfed by orange flames and thick black smoke. She ran several yards before crumbling to the ground. She and her baby burned to death before my very eyes. I was not more than a hundred yards away, and I could see the imprint of the baby on her back after both were dead. I looked at Richards and he looked at me. We both were thinking the same thing: If this guard shoots us, well, we deserve it because we should not be here in Korea.

This incident made me see the horror of war like nothing else. I had seen lots of deaths in combat, and somehow I could handle seeing a soldier get shot or even shooting one myself, but seeing innocent women and babies being killed really got to me. I was thinking, hell, if I die now, so what.

After the planes left, our guard kicked us a couple of times and signaled with his bayonet for us to get up and begin walking. We eventually reached the gathering point, where the Chinese had assembled hundreds of Americans and other UN prisoners. First they questioned the officers in a makeshift headquarters and then the rest of us. We knew we were supposed to give name, rank, and serial number, and nothing else. When I went in, I was not that frightened because so many others had already been questioned. Sitting in front of me were four Chinese intelligence officers, one of whom served as an interpreter and spoke perfect English. These four were professionals, not like the guy who told me I was the exploited. Hell, I think that guy only knew that one speech. The interpreter asked me what outfit I was in, but I refused to talk. I kept repeating, over and over again, name, rank, and serial number. Finally, he laughed and told me my outfit and even when I got to Korea. He said that our officers had already told them everything they wanted to know. I thought that was strange because, before I went in, one of the officers had whispered to me, "Don't tell them anything! Don't tell them anything!" I have to believe that some of these officers told the Chinese whatever they wanted to hear, and that made me lose all respect for them.

Frankly speaking, we enlisted men did not know anything. We did not even know where we were half the time. We could not give the enemy any information because we had nothing to give. We just took orders. And that's what I told the House Un-American Activities Committee in Washington after I returned to the States in 1966. I told the Committee, "We did not give any information because we knew nothing. We just fought and took orders. Only the officers had information to give."

· · · · · ★ · · · · ·

We stayed maybe two days at this gathering place for prisoners. Then the Chinese broke us down into groups and turned us over to the Korean People's Home Guard, which was supposed to march us northward to a permanent POW camp along the Yalu River. This was one of several infamous death marches that Allied prisoners were forced to make during the last half of 1950. We marched all day for ten days in sub-zero temperatures with little or no food and guarded by men who did not hesitate to shoot anyone who dropped out.

Already on the first day of the march I began to have physical problems. Before I was captured, my feet had gotten wet and frostbitten, and my right leg, from my foot almost up to my hip, was swollen. I had great trouble keeping up with the rest of the column. We were supposed to reach a specific destination each day by a certain time, and the guards became increasingly angry because I was slowing everybody down. In spite of the pain, I was determined to try and keep up because I had seen that those who did not just disappeared.

The guards would pull them out, and the rest of us would move on. Then we'd hear shots, so we knew what had happened. I am not sure why they did not shoot me, but maybe, just maybe, this was one of the very few times a black skin actually saved my life. I know that in the camps the instructors talked a lot about racism, so maybe the guards had orders to keep black prisoners alive.

During the second day of the march, I really slowed down. This one guard kept prodding me with his rifle to make me move faster, but I was now dragging my right leg because I could hardly move it. A white guy from New York, called Peach by most of us, came back to help me. I did not even know him. He was also wounded, having been shot through the shoulder. There was a small hole in front and a big one in back where the bullet exited, tearing the meat out with it. There were some black prisoners in our group, but none of them helped me. I was shocked when this white boy came back to help me. But the guard signaled him not to and began hitting him. I kept telling him, "Peach, go ahead. I can't keep up. There's no point in both of us getting killed. Just leave me." He tried to refuse, but I forced him to go on. The guard then pulled me aside and told me to wait. I figured this was it, that he was going to shoot me. He waited until the last soldier disappeared; then he signaled me to stand still and turned around and ran after the retreating column.

I just stood there and watched him disappear in the distance. I did not know what to do or where to go. It was at least twenty below zero, and I was freezing. I understood that without food or shelter I could not last more than a couple of days, so I knew I had to try and catch the other prisoners. I began walking in the direction the column had taken, and I walked until late that night, when all of a sudden a Korean came out of nowhere and pointed for me to leave the road and follow him down to this village where the rest of the guys were resting for the night.

When we got there, a guard came up to me and said, "You can't keep up."

I told him, "Yes I can. I can keep up."

He said, "No, you're slowing us down." He gave me a rice ball about the size of a tennis ball. In the center was some kind of bean paste. He also gave me a cup of hot water. Then he told me to start walking and pointed in the direction the column would be marching the next day. He also told me the only thing I could ask the Korean civilians for was water. If I asked them for anything else, they had orders to shoot me.

I could do that. I knew that *Mool ju she yoh* meant "Water, please." I ate the rice ball and started down the road. I walked all the rest of that night. As the sun rose the next morning, the column caught up and passed me and soon moved out of sight. Once more I was all alone. This went on for three days and three nights. I would catch up with them, get my daily rice ball and hot water, and then start out again. Sometimes, when I could see that the path was snaking back and forth down the mountain, I would just sit and slide down the hill to shorten the distance. And when I became too exhausted to move my feet, I just crawled on my hands and knees to give my frozen feet a rest.

I became so desperate this one day that I almost killed myself. I was crossing a river when I was overcome by exhaustion and hunger. I was sure I could not go on. I sat down on the edge of the bridge, and when I stared down at the frozen river, I saw my mother decked out in a beautiful dress, dancing on the ice. She motioned for me to come down and join her. It was like a beautiful dream, and I began inching forward toward the edge of the bridge. Just as I was about to fall, I snapped back into consciousness, and the vision disappeared. At that moment I understood how close I had come to death, but I also realized how much I wanted to live.

On the fourth or fifth day I was making my way as best I could when a Korean boy and girl, maybe five or six years old, came out of a village and began walking in front of me. Each was carrying a small sack with a string tied around it. There they were, all by themselves, walking in the same direction I was. When they saw me, they slowed down, but when I would almost catch up, they would run on ahead. They never let me catch them, but they kept looking back to see where I was. We walked like this all day. From time to time they opened their bags and ate some kind of parched grain, which might have been millet. They noticed I was looking at them while they were eating. So they put a few grains on a rock and ran off. When they looked back and saw me eating what they had left, they smiled and moved on. Maybe an hour later they ate some more and again left me a few grains. I picked them up and waved thanks to them. Those mountain roads were icy, and I was afraid they might slip and fall down the hillside. This really worried me, so I tried my best to keep up so I could possibly help them if they got in trouble. If something happened to those two kids, what would the Koreans think? I was so worried about protecting them that I was actually relieved when they finally left the road to go into another village, and we waved good-bye to each other.

On the far side of that village, I caught up with the other prisoners. Again, a guard pulled me off the road and fed me, but my right foot had become even worse. When my foot thawed out from frostbite, it began to blister and break open, and rubbing against the boot so irritated it that I could no longer pull on my boot. The guards let me rest until almost daybreak because they knew I had been out there a long time. We were sleeping in huts with Korean families. They'd pack as many of us in a room as they could, and the Koreans would keep watch over us. The guys in my room became angry with me when I took my boot off because my foot smelled so bad. We left before sunup the next morning. I had wrapped my foot in some rags I had found and carried my boot over my shoulder. When the sun came out, and the ice began to melt, the wrapping around my foot became wet. Then, when the sun went down, it froze to my foot and I could not get it off. I knew if I stopped, my foot would freeze solid, so I just kept walking. I could make it up the mountains, but the pressure of trying to slow myself going down really hurt. When I finally caught up to where the column had stopped to rest, the guards still refused to allow me to join them. They gave me a little time to rest and fed me a rice ball and my cup of hot water; then I had to hit the road again.

On, I think, the sixth day of the march I again thought I was going to die. I was still walking alone and had just come around a curve when I saw maybe fifteen Korean teenagers lined up on both sides of the road. As I approached them, I knew that something bad was going to happen. I tried to walk around them, but one of them came over and pulled me back and made me walk between them. After I walked past them, they grabbed me and made me do it again. Then it began to get rough. They began shoving me back and forth from one side of the road to the other. I'd get to the end, and they'd pull me back and make me do it over again. I decided to sing a familiar Korean song I had learned when I was stationed in Korea in 1947. It had a cheerful melody, and I even tried feebly to dance to it. They began laughing, but they also got rougher and rougher. And the more they shoved me back and forth, the more excited they became. Whatever they were going to do, I figured it would all be over soon. There was no way I could stop them, and I was far too weak to fight. I hoped that whatever they were going to do to me would happen quickly. I just wanted to get it over with.

At that moment, an old Korean with a long, stringy white beard came out of nowhere. He waved his cane in the air and shouted something at these kids, and they took off. Then he disappeared, and I just walked on. Thinking back on this experience, maybe I was being compensated for having saved that old man's life in Japan when Aggie John wanted to beat him to death.

Later that afternoon, or maybe it was the next day, I recall being very thirsty and walking up to this Korean house and asking the woman in Korean, *Mool ju she yoh*. She motioned me inside while she went in back to get me some water. There is a little section in the front of a Korean house where they cooked, and I noticed that she had some corn mush bubbling away in a big wok. I was really hungry, so when she went in the back to dip me some water, I reached into that wok and grabbed a handful of corn mush. It was scalding hot, so I jerked my hand out and put it inside my jacket, but a little corn stuck to my hand. I quickly drank the water and got out of there because my hand was burning. After I got down the road, the corn had dried, and the skin was coming off my hand, but I ate every grain, skin and all. If that old lady had seen me stealing that corn, she probably would have shot me.

We were finally approaching the end of the march. My foot was not any better, but either because my tenacity had impressed the guards, or maybe because we were ahead of schedule, I had managed to convince them that I could stay with the column for the rest of the way. We learned at the end of that day that we had only about five miles to go before we reached Pyuktong and the permanent compound, which was Camp 5. Our guards let us rest longer than usual that night. The next day they made us straighten up and march smartly through the village of Pyuktong. They even ordered our sergeants to count cadence. I guess they wanted us to look like we were real soldiers who had been treated well on the march.

CHAPTER FOUR

Camp 5

On December 10, 1950, approximately five hundred of us arrived at Camp 5, which was located on a peninsula just outside the town of Pyuktong, on the Yalu River, which separates North Korea from China. It was a beautiful spot, but not if you were a POW. The camp would eventually hold several thousand United Nations prisoners, including British, Turks, Australians, Filipinos, Puerto Ricans, and Americans, both black and white. At that time the camp was run by North Korean civilians with a couple of North Korean officers in charge. Later, the Chinese took over.

We had been told that when we arrived at our permanent camp, there would be hot food, warm buildings to sleep in, and the wounded would be taken care of, but we found just the opposite. There were no hot meals, no beds, no blankets, and no medicine. Twenty-five POWs were packed in an eight-by-ten-foot room in a small hut. Because there was not enough space for everyone to lie down, our legs would stretch over each other's chests. The air smelled so bad that when it was my turn to lie down, I put my nose to a small hole in the wall to get some fresh air. After all the promises of good conditions, this was a bitter disappointment, but war is war.

Almost immediately, prisoners began to die. The first to die were those with untreated wounds. With no medicine, there was nothing we could do for them. They just died. The next group died from malnutrition. They simply starved to death. Then disease took others. We had dysentery, often from drinking bad water. You could not walk anywhere without stepping in feces. We dug a slit trench with two logs alongside it, and we'd try to sit on the logs.

For the first time in my life, I felt I was being treated as an equal rather than as an outcast.
—Clarence Adams

Camp 5, located on the Yalu River near Pyuktong, North Korea. This photograph was probably taken by Frank "Pappy" Noel, a well-known AP photographer and POW. The Chinese allowed Noel to take several carefully screened photographs. Hundreds of Americans lay buried on the hillside above the camp. Photo courtesy of the National POW Museum, Andersonville National Historic Site, Andersonville, Georgia.

One guy fell in and no one had the strength to pull him out. By this time we had lost so much weight, we were too weak to do much of anything. I had dropped down to about ninety pounds.

We lost men who went outside the huts to relieve themselves. Often they were too weak to make it to the latrine areas, and we'd find them later frozen, just outside the building. Thirsty men also died when they ate contaminated snow because they either refused or were physically unable to walk away from the living areas to find clean snow.

Some of our guys were virtually eaten alive by lice. These hog lice were as big as soybeans, and they sucked your blood. We'd remove the shirt off some guy who had just died and we'd see his body just covered with lice. These were usually guys who were so badly wounded they could not pick the lice off themselves. I'd get a buddy to pick the lice off of me and then I would do the same thing for him. You had to pull them off carefully because the head was buried

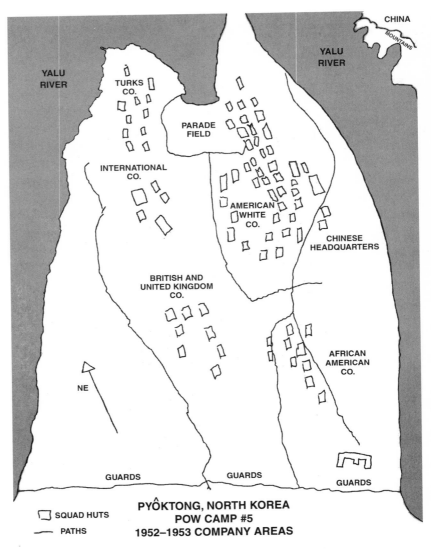

CHINA

YALU
RIVER

YALU
RIVER

TURKS
CO.

PARADE
FIELD

INTERNATIONAL
CO.

AMERICAN
WHITE
CO.

CHINESE
HEADQUARTERS

BRITISH AND
UNITED KINGDOM
CO.

AFRICAN
AMERICAN
CO.

NE

GUARDS

GUARDS

GUARDS

⬛ SQUAD HUTS
— PATHS

**PYÔKTONG, NORTH KOREA
POW CAMP #5
1952–1953 COMPANY AREAS**

*A rough drawing of Camp 5 made by fellow prisoner Richard M. Bassett
and used with his permission.*

under your skin, and if you broke it off, it would become infected. When you mashed a louse between your fingers, you'd hear a popping sound and see the blood running down your fingers.

I managed to find Peach the second week we were in Camp 5. I wanted to thank him for trying to help me on the march, but he was dying. His shoulder wound had become badly infected, and the pus was just oozing out. Every day I went to his hut, held him in my arms, and squeezed the pus out of his wound. We both knew he was going to die, but I did everything I could for him. We never even asked each other our full names. Under such circumstances, names were not important. He lasted two weeks, and we buried him on the hillside with the rest.

We made stretchers out of tree limbs and rope. The men on the daily burial details would carry the dead up the hill and throw them into these shallow mass graves and cover them with snow. Everyone was so weak that it took four people to carry one body. Sometimes one of the four carriers would die on the way, so we'd just pile his body on top of the first corpse, and the remaining three of us had to bury both of them, one on top of the other. I remember one fellow was too big for the burial trench. I lowered him in the ground and covered him with snow, but when I walked away, I made the mistake of looking back. One arm was sticking up. I went back, pushed it down, and packed more snow on it so it would not come up again. I again walked away, but when I looked back this time, I saw his leg had popped out. I felt so bad I went back and stepped on his leg, trying to push it down under the snow. After that, I did not look back anymore. When summer arrived, the Chinese bulldozed that whole area and covered everything up.

Our daily food ration when we arrived in Camp 5 consisted of a cup of hot water and maybe a quarter cup of uncooked corn, beans, or sorghum. I remember one Midwesterner complaining, "That's what we feed our farm animals." Nevertheless, this daily ration was divided up literally grain by grain by the "spoon man," who was elected and trusted by the rest of us. Nevertheless, hungry eyes scrutinized his every hand movement. When some guys said they could not eat this uncooked grain, I looked at them like they were crazy. Many of them were city boys, and most of them were white. They talked about eating things back home like chocolate éclairs. Hell, I didn't even know what a chocolate éclair was. I'd tell them, "If you want to live, you got to eat what they give us." They still insisted they could not. They simply gave up their will to eat, and within a few days they died.

I am sure the difficult conditions most blacks, and some poor whites, encountered back home helped us survive. I know I was determined to live. So I chewed and swallowed every grain of my daily ration. It tasted terrible, but it sustained life. Some of the guys would eat part of their ration, saving the rest for later, but this was not smart because once it became dark, those who did not give a damn would steal anything they could get their hands on.

In order to get extra rations, we often kept the bodies of dead prisoners in our room as long as possible. I remember setting corpses up against the wall for the daily head count. Living under such conditions, we begin to lose any feelings for others. We would fight viciously for any scrap of food and strip the dead of their clothing, boots, and anything else that might help the rest of us survive.

At first, black and white soldiers were put together in the same camp area and even the same rooms, but sometimes this resulted in racial conflicts. Aggie was a black seventeen-year-old who had been hit in both legs by American planes on the march. His wounds had become badly infected, and the discharge smelled terrible. A white guy who slept next to him became angry about the stench and called him "a filthy nigger." He then began kicking his wounded legs. The black soldiers in the room were furious. One of them shouted at him, "Why are you doing that? You know he's not going to make it." Later that night I heard someone crawl over me and jump this white prisoner. I could hear them struggling. The next morning we found the white guy dead on the floor. Aggie was also dead.

There were only 120 blacks in the entire camp, but we fared much better than the whites. Most of us were more accustomed to getting along on very little. I also think blacks stuck together better than whites, again because we were used to adversity. To make matters worse, many of the whites had been replacement troops and did not really know the other guys in their unit, but that never mattered to us blacks. We just accepted everyone, regardless of unit.

There was one Korean doctor in our camp. He had no medicine, but he'd come around for checkups every morning. He'd ask, "Peoki?" which meant, "Are you sick?" We were afraid to tell him we were *peoki* because then he'd say, "You need fresh air," and he'd order the guards to drag you outside. If you were put out in that freezing weather, you died. Even if somebody dragged you back in, it would often be too late. Pneumonia killed a lot of our guys.

Life continued like this for many months. Except for my turn on burial detail, I just sat or lay there on that cold earthen floor, staring into emptiness, wondering what I had done to deserve this terrible fate. But when spring finally came and the ground began to thaw, I became more active. Several of us began digging for roots. We tried to eat everything we found, and some plants proved edible. My favorite had four or five small, starchy lumps on its roots that tasted slightly sweet, like coconut. Anytime that I could dig up a handful of these roots was a good day for me.

The infection in my right foot became worse that first spring, and my toes began to turn green. I could see the bones poking through the skin, and the smell was horrible. Somebody told me that maggots would eat dead flesh and help heal the wound, so I got a dozen or so maggots from the wound of another prisoner and put them on my foot. I watched these white worms wiggling inside my wounds for days before I became so disgusted that I had to get rid of them. I knew I had to do something even more drastic or I was going to lose my entire foot and maybe even my leg. I decided to cut off the toes with gangrene at the first joint. Because my toes had rotted so badly, I could pretty much see where the joints were. I did not have a knife, so I made one out of the steel arch support from my combat boot. I sharpened it and scraped my toes to the bone. Then I counted to ten and cut two of them off at a time. Actually, I counted to ten about twenty times. I'd keep telling myself, "Just count to ten and do it." But when I'd get to ten, I'd start over again. Finally, I put the knife where I figured the joint was, counted to ten one last time, looked away, and cut the toes off at the joint. After I did my toes, I helped some of the other guys do theirs.

Somebody told me that sunlight killed germs and helped the healing process, so I exposed my foot to hours in the hot sun. It took almost a year for my foot to heal completely, but in the meantime I became more and more physically active. I ran, did pushups and pull-ups and all kinds of exercises to rebuild my body. I even began to box again.

The Chinese took over Camp 5 in the spring of 1951 and introduced what they called their "lenient policy." They lined us all up and told us that although they were not bound by the Geneva Convention, they had their own policy of leniency that would greatly improve our lives in the camp. We were skeptical, but we also knew that things could not get any worse. Nothing happened immediately, but after a couple of weeks, when the ice on the river began breaking up, a boat came down the Yalu River. It was a small boat, but it was loaded with rice and millet. The Chinese then set up a kitchen, and for the first time we got a bowl of hot food every day. They also assured us that as time went on, everything would get better, and gradually it did.

Sometime in the winter of 1951–52 the Chinese told us to burn our lice-infested army-issue clothing and gave us new clothes, toothbrushes, and soap. They also provided razors for those who wanted to shave.

Our sleeping conditions also improved. We were still sleeping in these small huts, which usually consisted of three rooms. The building was supposed to be heated by tunnels under the floor, but that first winter we did not have the strength to go out and gather wood, so we just slept on the cold floors. The Chinese now told us we had to gather wood for the coming winter. Those of us who were getting stronger welcomed the chance to get out of camp and go into the hills to gather wood. We'd start our fire during the day, and the heat would go through these tunnels. We'd bank the fire at night, but those floors would stay warm until morning. The hut was small enough so that just a few sticks would quickly heat up the floors. Sometimes the floors would get so hot, you could not lie on them until they cooled down. And because so many guys died that first winter, we now had more room. We still did not have beds, so our hips had big sores from sleeping on those hard floors. Not until long after liberation did those marks finally disappear.

On these wood-gathering details we discovered great patches of marijuana growing wild on the hillsides. We brought it back to the camp, ripped the wallpaper off our room, tore it into proper sizes, rolled up the marijuana, and made what we called "bombs." Some of these bombs were as big as the paper horns used to celebrate New Year's Eve, and their soothing effect provided an escape from the harsh reality of prison life. Marijuana also gave some of the guys a better appetite so they could eat their daily food ration.

With the improved conditions, the death rate gradually slowed down to almost nothing; in fact, the only death I remember during our last year and a half was a guy killed by lightning. He had to go outside to go to the bathroom during a severe thunderstorm. I told him to wait, but he said he couldn't. Shortly after he walked out the door, we heard a large boom. When we went outside to look, we discovered he had been struck by lightning. It had broken every bone in his body and even melted a G.I. metal spoon he carried in his pocket.

Owing to malnutrition and debilitating conditions during that first year of captivity, sex never was on our minds. But after our physical condition began to improve, women again became a daily topic, just as they were when we were soldiers back in our army barracks. Each morning after breakfast, most of us expectantly sat on our little stools facing south. Around ten o'clock a young Korean girl would appear on the hill overlooking the camp. She wore a plain army uniform and had long pigtails. We would watch her walking along the path leading up to a Buddhist temple that had been turned into some kind of public building, where she obviously worked. Each time she showed up, we would exclaim, "Here comes our dessert!" We would not start our daily routine until she disappeared into the temple.

One day several of us were unloading a supply boat on the Yalu River, and we spotted some Chinese women on the other side of the river washing clothes. We waved and shouted at them and decided to swim over for a closer look. We had just started toward them when one of the guards yelled at us to stop. I guess he thought we were trying to escape. We kept right on swimming, so he fired several warning shots into the river. When we saw bullets splashing all around us, we turned around and swam back. I had been out there too long and barely made it back to shore. I did not try that foolishness again.

Another time, we were sitting on the bank of the river when we noticed an American prisoner in the water, bobbing up and down and hollering for help. Nobody wanted to jump in and save him. I had never been a lifeguard, but when no one swam out to rescue him, I had to try to help him. I was afraid to get too close to him because he might grab me and pull me under, so I dived under him and grabbed him by the feet and began pushing him out of the water toward the bank. Every time I pushed him upwards, I went down deeper. So while he was going forward, I was going backward. The last time I pushed him, he landed right on shore. By this time I was out of breath and half drowned myself. When I sat down beside him, he looked at me but did not say a word. I tried to talk to him, but he refused to say anything. From that day on, he never spoke to me. I have no idea why he hated me so. I had never done anything to him except save his life. Maybe he resented that a black American had saved his life. I guess he wanted somebody else to save him.

There was racism in the prison camps just as there had been in the army. There were still those whites who openly called us niggers and told us what they would do to us when they got us back in the States. Whenever I encountered one of these guys, I thought to myself, And we're supposed to fight side-by-side with these crackers? I remember this white prisoner coming up to me in Camp 5 and saying, "Nigger, if I had you back home, you wouldn't talk to me like this."

I told him, "Yeah, but you ain't home. You're a stinking prisoner just like me," and I hit him upside the head. He might have believed he was going to do all kinds of things to me if he had me back in the States, but I showed him that as prisoners, we were all equal.

The Chinese told me they did not understand how, even under the most adverse of conditions, this racial hatred and inability to cooperate with one another still dominated so many white Americans. The Chinese cited this as one of the reasons they eventually separated white and black prisoners.

· · · · · ★ · · · · ·

The Chinese started our education classes in 1951. They began with long, tedious lectures that everyone had to attend. They taught us about imperialism and about who started the war, after which they would send us back to our huts to discuss the lectures. Initially I thought these lectures were total nonsense, so, like the rest of the guys, I just returned to my room and went to sleep. It was only when some of the American-educated lecturers talked about specific conditions in the States, such as racism, that I became interested. Of course, I knew nothing about communism or any other "-ism," but during many of my sleepless nights, I again questioned why America was in Korea and what I was doing there. The more I thought about my life, the more I felt I had been used, cheated, and betrayed.

I must admit the thought of never being able to go home again terrified me. New prisoners kept coming in, and with each new batch the hope that we would soon be liberated faded away. I began to think that the Chinese might be telling the truth, that we were actually losing the war. Looking back, I realize that it was then that some of the Communist propaganda began to sink in. More and more I asked myself, Who really benefits from this war? Is it the arms makers? The Chinese insisted it was a "rich man's war but a poor man's fight." It all sounded so elementary when the Chinese told us, "The capitalists on Wall Street started this war to sell their arms and to gain markets and raw materials in Asia."

When I thought about my life as a young black man, I had great difficulty in seeing what democracy and freedom had done for me. I thought back on that cold November day when my regiment was sacrificed for the sake of protecting the white units. I also recalled one hot afternoon when I was twelve and was beaten up by a white man at a gas station for no reason at all. And there were so many other indignities I had suffered growing up in Memphis. Such thinking led to more questions: Why are the rich rich and the poor poor? Why do blacks always get kicked around like animals? Of course, the Communists' answers to such questions were remarkably simple, and almost too obvious. The more I thought about all this, the more I believed there was some truth in what the Chinese were telling us. Critics in America later called this brainwashing, but how can it be brainwashing if someone is telling you something you already know is true?

The Chinese told us they were not going to do anything for us unless we were willing to cooperate. They said, "We do not understand the American way of life, so we need some volunteers to work with us." They asked us to select what they called monitors who would help them manage the camp and tell them what we needed. Each hut was to select a representative. No one wanted to be this go-between because we still considered the Chinese to be the enemy, and we did not want to be collaborators.

The Chinese again warned us, "If you do not send someone to represent you, we cannot do anything for you." We talked this over in our hut and selected Corporal Purvis D. Webster, an older black guy, who was a marvelous storyteller and respected by everyone. However, he refused because he feared that under the military's code of conduct, this would be considered collaboration and might result in a court-martial. But we were at a point where we had to decide if we wanted to live. I told myself, You've done all you can do. You fought and are damn lucky to be alive. Now that you are out of the war, you have to take care of Number One. At that point I was not particularly concerned about any code of conduct. I figured somebody had to cooperate if we were going to get out of there alive. To those who insisted we do nothing to help ourselves, my answer was, "It is far easier to give up and die than it is to live and die." After all, it was not like I had run away from the fields of battle. I had fought to the bitter end, but we had lost, and I got captured. The American government and its military could not help us now. We had to care for ourselves, and I thought I might be able to help. So I volunteered. The others told me, "Hey, you do this, but don't worry. We'll protect you. When we get back to America, we'll explain that you did this for us." Unfortunately, that did not happen.

At first, the Chinese did not trust me. They thought I was trying to spy on them. They made me write my autobiography, and they made me write it at least four times before they accepted it. They did not believe I was as poor as I told them I was. They thought every American had bacon and eggs for breakfast. When I wrote that for breakfast we had leftovers from supper, they insisted, "No! Americans eat bacon and eggs and sausage and toast for breakfast."

I told them, "No, only people with money eat like that." They thought I was lying so I could get their sympathy, but I was telling the truth. I kept writing the same thing over and over until finally they believed my story.

After the Chinese accepted me, they told me to write down what we wanted for improvements. I asked for a lot of things for the entire camp and not just the guys in my hut. I asked for sports equipment and permission to use an old building to set up a recreational facility. I told them some of the guys wanted a place where they could hold church services on Sunday morning. I also asked if we could let our cooks prepare the little food they gave us the way we liked it. Finally, I asked for better sanitary conditions and if we could have a library with books and newspapers.

To everyone's surprise, the Chinese agreed to everything I asked for. After a couple of months, they brought in bats and baseballs, footballs, books, boxing gloves, parallel bars, and a table game remarkably similar to pool. We set up cooking and sanitation committees. We exercised every day. And the guys began to get stronger. We even got some medicine that we gave to the prisoners who were medics to administer to the guys who really needed it.

I personally was put in charge of the library, which contained more than a thousand books and served all of the UN prisoners in Camp 5. Of course, the books were carefully selected by the Chinese. Most were by Russian and Chinese writers, such as Maxim Gorky and Lu Xun. Among the few Western authors were Charles Dickens, Mark Twain, Jack London, and W. E. B. Du Bois, whom I later met in China. The Chinese considered these writers to be Progressives who exposed the dark side of capitalism. Out of sheer boredom, I read nearly every book in the library, although I had never been much of a reader growing up.

We had Americans in Camp 5 who literally could not read or write. Some of the better-educated prisoners set up study groups that did such a good job of teaching that these former illiterates returned home with more education than when they entered the army.

The Chinese also set up voluntary study groups. Out of curiosity I joined one of them. By this time I had read several books about China and Russia and the new societies they were trying to build. I was introduced to the basics of Marxism and something called the history of social development. I also learned the difference between Chinese and Russian communism — and there certainly was a difference.

I was surprised that most of the Chinese instructors were not army officers but professors, editors, or top officials from various organizations. Some of them even had American college degrees. For the most part they were friendly and personable, and they greatly impressed me when they insisted there was no discrimination in China. They told me that for the first time, poor and disadvantaged people had access to higher education and could become doctors, engineers, and top officials in the government. I was fascinated by what seemed to me to be a totally revolutionary society.

I still have my small notebook where I wrote down the names of the Chi-

Clarence Adams and William C. White standing in front of the Camp 5 activities building Adams helped negotiate with the Chinese. This photo appeared in United Nations P.O.W.'s in Korea, *which was published by the Chinese for worldwide distribution.*

nese instructors who made an impression on me. I cannot remember all of them, but Instructors Lu and Yee were particularly noteworthy; in fact, I spent more time with Instructor Lu than anyone else. Neither of these men had been to America, so they had obviously learned their English in China. Their written English was very good, and after they spent time with us, their spoken English became much better.

In addition to my library responsibilities, I headed up the mess and recreation committees. After some additional instruction, I was also appointed a monitor and gave lectures on feudalism, slavery, imperialism, capitalism, social development, and the accumulation of wealth. By then, of course, I had become very Progressive. I also became a regular contributor to the camp propaganda newspaper, *Toward Truth and Peace.* As a result, I had made some friends but also some dangerous enemies. After they returned to the States, some of the latter said I had harmed them, but I never harmed a soul. In truth, I actually worked hard on behalf of all prisoners.

· · · · · ★ · · · · ·

In January 1951 the Chinese launched their so-called Peace Movement. They began by asking prisoners in all the prison camps to sign the Stockholm Peace Appeal, which called for an end to all hostilities. Almost three hundred of us signed this appeal. We were also told to write home asking our families and friends to help stop this bloody war. I sincerely believed in this campaign and actively participated. I wrote the Reverend S. A. Owen of the Memphis Metropolitan Baptist Church and asked him to pray for world peace. I found out later he read my letter aloud to the congregation.

In the spring of 1952 I also signed a petition against germ warfare after talking to a couple of captured American pilots who had flown such missions. I even gave lectures on this to other prisoners. I pointed out the hypocrisy of always accusing our enemies of war atrocities when we too often have been guilty of doing the same thing.

I do not know whether I was deluding myself or not, but I felt my efforts were helping to bring about world peace. In no way did I think I was betraying my country. To the contrary, I thought I was doing everything I could to help the cause of peace. This gave me a sense of mission I had never felt before. It was like being a part of something much greater than my own life.

When the negotiations dragged on and on, primarily over the issue of repatriation, several of the Progressives signed a letter to the United Nations pleading with its General Assembly to speed up the negotiations and bring an end to the war:

To: Representatives of all countries in the United Nations General
    Assembly
From: POW Camp, Democratic People's Republic of Korea,
    February 22, 1953

Dear Sirs:
We, the undersigned, have been prisoners of war for over two years. During these two years our welfare has never been neglected and our stay here has been made as comfortable as possible. But personal comfort can never substitute for the yearning which we all have to return to our families and our natural desire to return home still remains in spite of the fact that we are being treated well and living comfortably.

We have been closely following the Korean Armistice Negotiations with the hope that those negotiations would arrive at a successful settlement of the Korean Question, but so far our hopes and desires have not been realized.

Since the repatriation of POWs is to be discussed during the seventh session of the General Assembly to be held February this year, we wish to appeal to all the members of the General Assembly to do everything within your power to settle the issue of the repatriation of prisoners of war as soon as possible so that we may return to our homes in the shortest possible time.

We think that the only possible way of settling this issue is to cease hostilities immediately and adhere to the practice of International Law and the Geneva Convention on the total repatriation of prisoners of war. Only in this way can our hopes and desires of returning home be fulfilled.

We remain, yours truly, . . .[1]

$$\cdots\cdots \bigstar \cdots\cdots$$

I never became a Communist or a Chinese citizen, not even after my many years in China. I was looking for something much more fundamental. I wanted to be treated as a human being, and I wanted the opportunity to live a better life. Although our Chinese captors never became close to any prisoners, they at least treated black and white prisoners with equal dignity—or indifference. Thus, for the first time in my life, I felt I was being treated as an equal rather than as an outcast.

William C. White and Larance V. Sullivan were two other black prisoners who belonged to my study group. They also later joined me and the other eighteen in refusing repatriation. Sullivan had such a good voice that he had performed the weekly Gospel readings in his church back home in Plumerville, Arkansas. As a result, the Chinese made him the PA announcer. Every day, Sullivan's deep and resonant voice filled the morning air as he read passages from one of several powerful anticapitalist texts.

Many of the white prisoners noticed this change in attitude that we three black Progressives no longer hid. They still referred to us as "niggers," but now they openly stated that we would never get back to the States alive, or if we did, they'd look us up and take care of us then. Of course, I already had made many enemies, and some of them, mostly white, had previously threatened my life. Since the murder of the white prisoner who slept in my room, I always tried to keep awake at night and sleep during the day. To this very day, more than forty years after the war, my wife never touches me while I'm asleep. More than once I have jumped out of a deep sleep in the middle of a nightmare and taken a swing at anyone near me.

Many of those whites who despised me and considered me a Commie nevertheless were quite willing to accept what I was able to do for them. No matter how much they hated me, they also understood that I had helped get improvements that made life better for everybody. Somebody had to make the sacrifice, and I did it. In the beginning it was primarily for myself, but later everyone enjoyed the benefits, and life in the camp got better.[2]

I did have some friends among the other prisoners, but not many. Most of them were black, but there were also some blacks who hated my guts, and they threatened me just like the white prisoners did. I became close friends with two blacks from Memphis. Neither was a Progressive, but they trusted and protected me. We called ourselves the Boys from the Big M. By this time I was sleeping in the library, and they would sometimes stand guard by the door while I slept. I told them, "When we get home, we will pool our army back pay and open a small shop." I had learned from the Chinese that the capitalists get rich because they own the means of production, so I told my buddies, "Let's own our own means of production."

I continued to do what I thought was right. After that first winter, most of the POWs continued to blame the Chinese for the deaths in the camps, but I could no longer do that. First of all, our instructors also had very little to eat, and the Koreans down in the village had practically no food. We were prisoners, so why should we get more to eat than those people had? We were the ones who had destroyed everything. The Chinese told the truth when they said they could not get supplies to the prison camps because the U.S. Air Force was bombing the supply routes. The Chinese cadres running Camp 5 would tell us, "We're hungry too," and we could see that they were. In war, if anybody is going to eat, it is going to be the captors, not the captives. I told the guys, "Hey, we can't blame the Chinese. We've got to blame our friends for doing too good a job on the supply lines." When I tried to get some of the prisoners to understand this, many of them became even more angry with me.

As I look back on all this, and I have been doing so for many years, the Chinese and the North Koreans did the best they could for us in the prison camps. You have to look at the circumstances. It was war, and war is a cruel thing. Some of the guys returned home and said they were physically tortured, but I never saw this happen. People ask me even now, "Hey, when you were a POW, did they torture you?" Not even the North Koreans overtly tortured us, although they certainly did shoot stragglers on those long death marches, and they quite willingly left us to die in the camps. But I never saw the kind of blatant torture you so often see in Hollywood's simplistic war movies.

Sometimes we were punished. I was myself. There was a warehouse in Camp 5 where they kept grain. There was a small opening on one side of the building that looked like a rat hole. When I stuck my finger in, I felt a burlap bag that had rice in it. I took a stick and poked a hole in the bag, and the rice poured out into my hand. When I got caught, the Chinese punished me by making me stand on one foot, with a guard watching me to make sure I did so. If he saw me with two feet on the ground, he was supposed to shoot me. But you can stand on one foot for only so long. So when he wasn't looking, I switched feet. I did this for about an hour. Every time he looked away, I changed feet. I don't know why he never noticed what I was doing. Maybe he didn't want to.

We had guys try to escape, but they escaped for only an hour or two. There was simply nowhere to go. To the north was the Yalu River, and on the other side was China. And there was no way you could get far enough south to reach the UN lines. None of us looked Chinese or Korean. A black guy could be standing on top of a mountain, and someone would say, "Hey, there's a black guy up there." A white boy might get away a little longer, but not for more than a couple of hours. Where were you going to get something to eat? No one was going to help you. We were not stupid. We knew we would not have made it a mile without being spotted.

When the Chinese caught an escapee, they made him stand in front of everybody and criticize himself for trying to escape. Sometimes they'd put him in what we called the turnip bin, which was simply a hole in the ground where they kept him for a day or more.

On May 29, 1953, I received a letter from my mother. This was only the third letter I had received in the thirty months since my capture. It was a short letter, but I read and reread it many times. I felt terribly homesick. I wrote in my notebook, "On this Sunday, I am in good health, but my thoughts seem to be running wild. It has been a very long time. I have seen 130 Sundays like this, some filled with rain and some with sunshine, but they all add up to the same thing: thoughts of home and mother." I was so emotional that I copied my mother's letter into my notebook, including the envelope. At times like this I would have been better off if I had never received any letters from home.

The opening ceremonies of the Inter Camp Olympics. According to the official caption, "Column after column, 500 P.O.W. athletes of 11 nationalities enter the stadium to the strains of 'The March of Friendship.' " Photo is from the brochure "Inter Camp Olympics."

· · · · · ★ · · · · ·

A welcome interlude occurred in our daily lives with the Inter Camp P.O.W. Olympics, held November 15–27, 1952, in Pyuktong, just outside of Camp 5. This was a time of heated negotiations, and the Chinese obviously hoped to gain positive worldwide publicity for hosting these games. Some prisoners refused to participate, but others, including Progressives, Reactionaries, and those in between, welcomed this diversion from the tedium of their daily lives, as well as the chance to talk to buddies from other camps.

Some five hundred POWs, representing all the prison camps in North Korea, competed in a such events as football, baseball, softball, basketball, volleyball, track and field, soccer, gymnastics, and of course boxing, where I fought as a lightweight. We had our own photographers, announcers, and even reporters who put out a newspaper called the "Olympic Roundup" after each day's events. There was also a talent show, as well as an arts and crafts fair. It was great fun and made us forget about where we were for a least a few days.

Improvised boxing ring where Clarence Adams and many other prisoners fought their matches. Photo is from the brochure "Inter Camp Olympics."

· · · · · ★ · · · · ·

The issue that kept the war dragging on was voluntary versus involuntary repatriation.[3] Eventually, in July of 1953, the two sides signed the armistice agreement which gave prisoners the right to choose where they wanted to be repatriated. I really did not know what to do. Once we knew our liberation was near, we talked a lot about going home and what we would do after returning. Many of us even exchanged addresses and planned visits and reunions. But I was also continuing to receive threats on my life. One guy swore he was going to throw me overboard on the home-bound ship. I tried not to take this too seriously, because certain prisoners had been threatening me since I became a Progressive. I still felt I was tougher than any of them. Besides, there were many other so-called Pros, and I was certainly not the most "Progressive" American in camp.

Nevertheless, I knew I would face a court-martial and likely a dishonorable discharge, if not worse. Even if I escaped all that, I would once again have to start at the very bottom of society. I would suffer discrimination, and there would be little economic opportunity for a better life. By this time I had been around the Chinese long enough to begin to like and understand them, and I was curious whether communism really was as good inside China as our instructors insisted it was. One thing I did know for sure. I might not have known what China was really like before going there, but I certainly knew what life was like for blacks in America, and especially in Memphis.

I talked to one of the Chinese instructors about my concerns. He told me I did not have to go back to the States, that I could go to one of several neutral countries of my own choosing and settle there. I asked him if this list included China. He told me that because China was not a neutral country, he would have to ask his superiors.

The next day he told me I could indeed go to China, but that first I would be kept in a neutral zone for three months. There American authorities would have the right to talk with me, but after that, if I still wanted to go to China, I would be free to do so. This would come under the voluntary repatriation clause of the peace agreement.

I was delighted. When I asked him what I could do in China, he responded, "What do you want to do?" After a brief moment, I told him I wanted an education, a job, and to get married. He said, "We shall send you to one of our universities, after which you will certainly have a job." Then he laughed and said, "As for marriage, we have a lot of women in China, but it's up to you to find your own wife."

CHAPTER FIVE

Turncoat?

The news that twenty-one American prisoners of war had refused repatriation and were planning to take up residence in the People's Republic of China was truly shocking to the folks back home, who could easily understand thousands of Communist prisoners refusing to return to North Korea or the People's Republic of China but not American boys choosing Communism over Democracy.[1] U.S. News & World Report editorialized that these were men who had "ratted" on their comrades, "suffered unhappy home lives," and were "lacking in formal education."[2] Newsweek described the defectors as "the sorriest, most shifty-eyed and groveling bunch of chaps," asserting that "about half . . . were bound together more by homosexuality than Communism."[3] The Chicago Tribune's Colonel Robert McCormick contended that most of the defectors had come from the slums of New York, where "subversive European ideologies flourished."[4] Other periodicals suggested that they had been dope addicts, juvenile delinquents, adult criminals, products of left-wing schools, or were lacking in religious training. Even the Chicago Defender, a nationally distributed black newspaper, reported that "a United States source, close to the United Nations command, claims the twenty-two [sic] men were won over to the side of the Communists by offers of girls, wealth, and power."[5] Another African American newspaper, the Pittsburgh Courier, headlined, "Race POWs Stay with Communists.[6] Given the national political climate, major black newspapers such as the Defender, the Courier, and the Michigan Chronicle found communism to be a greater evil than racism. The mainstream white periodicals, such as U.S. News & World Report, insisted that "American Negro soldiers did not swallow the Communist line of racial equality,"[7] or if they did, as in the case of Clarence Adams, William White, and Larance Sullivan, it was not due to racism back home but because they had been brainwashed by the Communists.[8]

(The turncoats) were lonely, bitter men who felt betrayed by fellow Americans. They were in a mood to swallow the Communist line. . . . They were unable to acquire the self-discipline needed to resist despair in the prison camps. . . . All of them appeared sullen and shifty-eyed."
— U.S. News & World Report, December 25, 1953

I had to go to China for the right to create a good life. I should have been able to do this in my own country.
— Clarence Adams

In truth, the twenty-one were as varied as were their fellow prisoners who eagerly accepted repatriation. Eighteen had been Regular Army career soldiers. Three were African Americans. Among the others, one was born abroad, and another's parents were foreign-born. The rest were men of Anglo-Saxon or Irish stock whose families had been in the United States for generations. Three had attended college, and six were high school graduates. The majority were practicing Protestants or Catholics who came from small towns or rural America, but six grew up in large cities, such as Detroit, Baltimore, and, of course, Memphis. Several were products of broken homes or had lost a parent to death. Interestingly, none was political, with the possible exception of James Veneris, whose parents had been Communists in their native Greece. All were obviously angry or disappointed with something in their lives, but this also described hundreds of other POWs who chose not to remain behind. What was never mentioned in the press was that under the terms of the truce, all former prisoners had the right to choose any country that would take them. Of course, when the United States government agreed to these terms, it was thinking only of the thousands of prisoners the United Nations forces were holding in South Korea who did not want to return to their Communist homelands.

I never considered myself to be a "turncoat," because under the terms of the armistice I was entitled to be a free man who could live wherever he wished. I decided to go to China because I was looking for freedom and a way out of poverty, and I wanted to be treated like a human being instead of something subhuman. I never belonged to the Communist Party, I never became a Chinese citizen, and in no way did I betray my country.

My decision not to return to the U.S. was a difficult one, and I agonized over it for many sleepless nights. I constantly thought about home and my mother, but the America of my youth seemed so very far away. I had become a very different person, and an integral part of my worldview now included a growing understanding of class exploitation and a commitment to racial equality. I knew I would never be able to go back to my old life in Memphis. I naturally felt an uncertainty about a new life in China, but I also understood that my old life was a dead end.

Making my decision all the more difficult was the fact that several very good friends were going back to the States. These were buddies who, although not necessarily Progressives, respected our friendship and what I had tried to do in Camp 5. Several of them wrote final messages in my notebook:

To Clarence "King Fish" Adams:
Time, place, and the greatest of pleasure allowed me the opportunity to write this token of our undying friendship in your book. I have known you

for almost two years. To me you have been more than just a friend. You have been more like a lost brother with every day here drawing us closer together. I wish there was some way that we could meet again in the very near future, but since there isn't, let me be one to wish you good luck. May your every effort be crowned with success. Coming from a guy who thinks a helluva a lot of you.

Your friend always,
Thomas Grant

Friend Adams:
I have a profound respect for you, especially for your high hopes for our race to advance. Continue to walk on in that direction. Walk on, walk on, with hope in your heart, and you'll never walk alone. At the end of that road, may we meet. I should like to compare battle scars with you.

Your friend,
Ray Carter
2 June 1953

To King Fish:
Well partner the moment has come when we must part. I want you to know that we have enjoyed every moment of our friends. You are a true friend and true friendship is golden and one should treasure it. Wishing you all the happiness and success in the days to come.

Chuck Sherman Cross
Aug. 1, 1953

I had come to believe the Chinese instructors in Camp 5 when they told me that my life under communism would be much better than the one I had left behind. I had also read a lot about China in the camp library, and I wanted to experience communism and the Chinese way of life for myself. I fully understood that I was stepping into a vast unknown. What if I got there and found things to be really bad and that my life in China was no better than the one I had left behind in Memphis? This concern, however, did not mean I distrusted the Chinese or what the instructors had been telling me; but I wanted to see for myself. As I look back, after a half-century, I realize my desire for a better life was greater than any fears I might have had.

Many Americans thought the Chinese had somehow brainwashed us into going to China. Typical were the comments syndicated labor columnist Victor Riesel uttered in a speech in Dallas on April 15, 1954: "They were so thoroughly brainwashed in the prison camp three years ago that the phrases and shibboleths of Soviet jargon spill from their lips like mumbo-jumbo from the lips of the robots in George Orwell's 1984."[9] Nothing could have been further from the truth. In fact, at first, the Chinese did not trust me. No one said, "Okay, you can now go to China." They made me explain why I wanted to go, and they made me explain this over and over again before they agreed to accept me. Basically, each time I told them the same thing: "I do not want to go back to America because I am hoping for a better life than the one I left in the United States. The best I can ever hope for back home is to become a mail carrier or a schoolteacher, and even those jobs are few and far between, and my family is too poor for me to go to college."

I did not want to be the only black going to China, so I finally told William White and Larance Sullivan that I was not going home. I did not dare tell anybody else. I told White and Sullivan essentially the same thing I told the Chinese about seeking a better life in China than blacks could ever expect at home, and they agreed. I told them not to tell anybody, but rumors started circulating, and guys again threatened us. Nevertheless, no one knew for sure what we were going to do.

· · · · · ★ · · · · ·

On August 23, 1953, a ship docked on the Yalu River below Camp 5 to transport the UN prisoners on the first leg of their repatriation. When the POWs began to line up to board the ship, those of us not going were put on an army truck and taken to a nearby mountain. There we stood in silence and watched as the others boarded the ship and left the harbor. Only then did it really hit me that I had reached the point of no return.

Those of us who chose to stay were just ordinary working-class Americans. Three of us were black and the rest white. Not one of us came from the kind of wealthy family where someone could argue that we had been spoiled. Even the whites had not led that good a life before they went in the army. Several of us were high school dropouts, but six or seven had graduated from high school, and some had gone on to college. Whatever our formal education, we could all read and write and were capable of making our own decisions. Simply put, we were former POWs who had decided to do something different with our lives. We were open-minded, and obviously most of us had participated in Progressive activities in the prison camps; after all, the Chinese would not have allowed any Reactionaries to come to China. We were certainly not Communists; in fact, we knew nothing about communism, except what we heard in the lectures in Camp 5.

After we decided we were not going home, we jointly issued a statement to the media that I doubt many Americans ever had a chance to read:

> Our staying behind does not change the fact that we are Americans. We love our country and our people. Therefore we love personal freedom. Our greatest concern is to fight for peace and freedom, not only for ourselves but for the American people and people of the world.[10]

White, Sullivan, and I, of course, had our own reasons for going to China. We wanted to escape the racism we had suffered in our own country and in the military as well. We also wanted an education, a decent job, and to be treated with respect. Years later I had a chance to read about my decision in my hometown newspapers, but they never mentioned that I was looking for social justice and economic opportunities. Typical was the September 24, 1953, issue of the *Memphis Press-Scimitar*, which stated that I refused to come home because I had "chosen to go to the University of Peking in Red China to study the Marxist doctrine." When a local reporter asked my mother why I was not coming home, he reported her as saying, "I don't believe it—it's just another Communist trick. He wouldn't play with them. He loved his country too much for that. He was deeply religious and wouldn't accept any way of life that denies God."[11]

My mother was understandably upset about my decision not to come home. In early October she made a radio recording at WMPS, Memphis's ABC outlet, pleading with me to change my mind. She insisted, "They must have doped them or used hypnosis." Some of the parents of the others also made similar broadcasts over ABC outlets, but none of their comments ever reached us.[12]

· · · · · ★ · · · · ·

The Chinese brought the non-repatriates from the other camps to Camp 5 for an initial indoctrination. They began by asking us about our immediate needs. I did not ask for any material things, except for shoes, clothing, and a hat, because I wanted to get rid of my POW clothes. Some of the others also asked for watches and other nonessential items. The Chinese took our measurements and had Korean tailors make Western-style suits for us. In about a week we all had new clothes. They also took us to see Korean operas, put on banquets for us, and generally treated us very well.

The Chinese and North Koreans never called us Communists, but they now referred to us as Comrades and Fellow Fighters for Peace. However, we were not allowed immediately to go to China. The July 27, 1953, armistice agreement called for a Neutral Nations Repatriation Commission to administer a three-month waiting period, followed by a thirty-day grace period, in a neutral zone outside Kaesong, where we were to be interned. Initially there were twenty-seven or twenty-eight former UN prisoners, including a Scottish soldier and a British marine, but only twenty-one of us Americans actually ended up in China.

The Americans who refused repatriation were housed in a small area of the neutral zone that we called the Banana Camp because it was shaped like a banana. We were under the control of Indian soldiers, who were supposed to be neutral, but we were convinced that they were taking orders from Americans who were determined to stop us from going to China. The Chinese could send in food, but they were not allowed to have any direct contact with us. The Indians even mounted machine guns around the perimeter of the camp and threatened to shoot us if we tried to get out and contact the Chinese. However, we were determined to tell them what was happening, so we told the Indians that Sullivan was so sick that he had to go to the hospital. The Chinese had a plant among the hospital staff, and Sullivan was able to tell him what was going on inside the Banana Camp.

During our months in the neutral zone, "Explainers" from our respective countries were allowed to contact us about our decision not to return home. The American Explainers promised that if we changed our minds about going to China, even at the last minute, the army would not hold our initial decision against us. That clearly was a lie, because when Claude Batchelor changed his mind, after a fervent plea from his Japanese wife, he was court-martialed and sentenced to spend the rest of his life in prison.[13] When the rest of us learned what the military had done to Batchelor, we wrote a letter to his mother, which, among other things, said, "This trial and sentence of your son must go down as a black page in the history of American justice. After knowing your son as we have, and reviewing the particular conditions surrounding his trial, with its trumped-up charges, fixed jury, and atmosphere of hate and mistrust whipped up by the government through the press, we can only conclude that Claude was unjustly tried and for a definite political purpose."[14]

On January 23, 1954, the Explainers announced over a loudspeaker that this would be the final chance for the rest of us to change our minds. But when no one came forth, they left for good. Five days later a Major General William E. Bergin of the Office of the Adjutant General wrote a letter to my mother stating that any past government payments to her would now be reviewed.

Just hours after the Explainers left, so did the Indian soldiers. When I woke up the next morning, the camp was empty, the gates were wide open, and

DEPARTMENT OF THE ARMY
OFFICE OF THE ADJUTANT GENERAL
WASHINGTON 25, D. C.

IN REPLY REFER TO
AGPS-C 201 Adams, Clarence C.
RA 14 267 602 (23 Jan 54)

28 January 1954

Mrs. Gladys Peoples
1528 Doris Avenue
Memphis, Tennessee

Dear Mrs. Peoples:

The Secretary of the Army has asked me to inform you that a discharge which became effective 23 January 1954 has been issued for your son, Corporal Clarence C. Adams, who has elected to remain with his Communist captors.

The Commanding General, Army Finance Center, Indianapolis 49, Indiana, will communicate with you concerning any allotments which you may have been receiving during the period your son has been missing.

I realize the grief and anxiety that have been yours since your son was first reported missing in action and I regret that this sad news must be added to the burden you have so bravely borne.

Sincerely yours,

WM. E. BERGIN
Major General, USA
The Adjutant General

Attired in their new suits, Clarence Adams (sixth from left) and the other twenty former American POWs pose for a final photograph in Panmunjom before leaving for China.

the Chinese had moved in. A few days later they held a press conference at Panmunjom. We were all there in our new Western-style Korean-made suits, and each of us made a short speech. I remember jokingly telling the reporters, "I'm sure my future in China will be as bright as my new suit." A few days later, on February 24, 1954, we crossed into China on a special train, and our new lives began.

CHAPTER SIX

University Days: Beijing and Wuhan

When we arrived in Taiyuan, which is the capital of Shanxi Province in northern China, some 230 miles southwest of Beijing, we were met by the Red Cross Society, which was to be our official guardian the entire time we were in China. Its representatives took us to a compound where we were able to take a shower, after which we were the guests of honor at a tremendous banquet. In my entire life I have never seen so much food. There was a long table covered with everything you could imagine. We hadn't eaten well in several years, so it was difficult to handle such rich food. I wanted to eat everything on the table, but my stomach couldn't take it. I felt terrible because I couldn't eat more, but after a few bites, my appetite was gone.

The Red Cross asked us what we wanted to do in China. Some of the whites were looking for adventure, but the strangest request came from Lowell Skinner, who wanted to become a general. He figured that an American corporal was smarter than a Chinese general, so he told the Chinese, "Make me a general and give me some weapons." Skinner was kind of crazy. The rest of us just wanted to work for world peace and to become friends with the Chinese people.

The day after our great feast, we began briefings on what life would be like in China. Our instructors initially asked us to examine our past lives because the American lifestyle was so different from what we would find in China. They wanted us to comprehend these differences so we could learn to live in harmony with the Chinese people.

I was very impressed when I learned that the Chinese

My best years in China were my student years.
— Clarence Adams

government had taken prostitutes off the streets and reeducated them in reform centers. Those willing to change were given a chance to start a new life, and many did quite well in different professions. Some even managed to become high-ranking factory officials. I realized that they were making a point to us former soldiers, but they did it in a way that was not embarrassing to anyone.

After a couple of weeks, our guardians thought we were ready to be turned loose on the Chinese people. Of course, we were not going to do anything foolish. After all, there were a billion Chinese, and we were a handful of foreign guests. They gave us some spending money, and we were allowed go into town. The first thing we did was go into an ice cream and cookie shop. Most customers got a small scoop of ice cream in a tiny cup, but we had these washbasins we had been issued. We put them on the counter and said, "Fill 'em up!" The shop manager looked at us very strangely, especially after we bought all his ice cream and then added some cookies. I guess he thought we were crazy.

Most of the Chinese in Taiyuan were very friendly. They had seen lots of Russians, so they were accustomed to foreigners, but they were curious about who we were and what we were doing there. When I later traveled to more remote parts in the interior of China, I found people who had never seen foreigners.

After we finished this initial education and adjustment period, we had to make a decision about what kind of career we wanted to pursue. Basically, we could become students or work in factories or on farms. Some, like James Veneris and Howard Adams, chose factories because they had done that kind of work in the States. They were sent to Jinan, about three hundred miles south of Beijing. Others were sent to an auto repair shop in Hankou because they already had those kinds of skills. The nine of us who wanted to study were sent to the People's University in Beijing.

The school authorities in Beijing took good care of us. We had free medical care, and they even brought in a cook from Shanghai to prepare American food for us. We had English-speaking professors who taught us about the Chinese and Russian revolutions, the history of social and economic development, and of course the Chinese language. We could not continue on in college unless we first learned Chinese.

Chinese is not an easy language for Americans to learn. We are used to the letters of the alphabet, but now we had to learn a completely different way of speaking and writing. We started with phonetics and then moved on to learning the characters. Then we learned vocabulary and the forming of sentences.

Studying in Beijing. First row from left: Scott Rush and Andrew Fortuna; second row: Morris Wills, unknown woman, and Clarence Adams; back row: unknown man, Larance Sullivan, and Richard Corden.

When my understanding became good enough, I was allowed to attend regular lectures with the Chinese students. When I missed something or did not understand, my Chinese roommate or classmates would help me. I even learned to take notes in Chinese.

After I completed my two years of study in Beijing, I could speak some Chinese. At the very least, I could carry on a conversation and go on my own to town to shop and visit the teahouses. My Chinese sounded funny, but I could survive. I could also read and write a little, but this was still very difficult. Nevertheless, I was ready to take the next step in my education, which meant traveling some seven hundred miles south to the city of Wuhan in central China, where for the next five years I would study for my degree in Chinese literature.

Wuhan University was located on the side of a small mountain called Lo Gia San, overlooking Wuhan, a city of several million inhabitants. The natural environment around the school was extraordinarily beautiful. In the spring, when the cherry trees were in full bloom, the fragrance from the blossoms engulfed the entire area. At the foot of the mountain was East Lake, where I loved to take a pre-sunrise swim, when there was not even a ripple on the water. These were the happiest years of my life.

As beautiful and tranquil as East Lake was, I remember one frightening day when I almost drowned in its waters. Several of us swam into this huge bed of seaweed that we had no idea was there. It wrapped itself around our bodies like a giant octopus. The more we struggled, the harder it became to stay afloat. We must have been in it for a good fifteen or twenty minutes. Very slowly, we had to peel the seaweed off our arms and legs; otherwise it would have pulled us under. We did not have a boat with us, which was not very smart.

That experience brought back memories of another time I almost drowned. It was back in Camp 5 in North Korea. When the weather was warm, I loved to swim out into the Yalu River and dive down to the bottom. One afternoon I plunged too far into its depths and lost all sense of direction. I could no longer see the surface light and did not know which way was up. For a long time, I felt trapped and began to black out. I had pretty much resigned myself to dying when finally I felt the warmth of the surface waters and broke through into the air. The experience frightened me, but it also left me with the feeling that it was not yet my time to go.

I majored in Chinese language and literature at Wuhan, but in order to graduate, the university required that all students know two foreign languages. I tried to study Russian, but only for three months. I discovered that I could not learn two foreign languages simultaneously. I told the dean, "I simply do not have the time to study both Chinese and Russian because both are very, very difficult." Because I was a foreign student, he made an exception and let me drop Russian. I knew I was not going to live in Russia, but I was living in China, so I wanted to focus all my energies on Chinese.

I was also required to take courses in Marxism, Leninism, and Maoism, similar to those I had taken in Beijing. The regular Chinese students, in addition to their majors, were required to take these same courses, as were cadre members of the Communist Party, and I am sure they had to do this every year.

The courses on revolution and international affairs made a profound impression on me. I found the relationships among nations to be fascinating, especially how they allied with one another to fight wars and to protect their colonies. As a result, I became very involved in politics. I also became very idealistic and wanted to become a true leader for the people. At least, those were my thoughts when I decided to learn everything I could about politics.

I especially enjoyed the simplicity of Mao's writings. His thoughts were so down-to-earth. If you could read, you could understand what he was saying, and of course he greatly improved the literacy rate in China. For example, Mao wrote, "If you see the enemy and he's got a little gun, you match it, but if he's got a big gun, you have to get a bigger one still." That makes sense. If your enemy has a cannon, you do not go after him with a pistol. Mao also wrote, "We should support whatever the enemy opposes and oppose whatever the enemy supports." Again, this was simply common sense, as was his insistence that "an army without culture is a dull-witted army, and a dull-witted army cannot defeat the enemy."

To be sure, Mao's sayings were meant to politicize the workers and peasants, such as when he said, "All our literature and art are created for the workers, peasants, and soldiers and are for their use." But they were also meant to make the common people feel a part of their country and its institutions. I did not necessarily agree with everything Mao wrote, but I certainly admired the way he expressed himself.

Another great writer was Lu Xun, who wrote in the early twentieth century. He is considered the father of modern Chinese literature because he wrote in the everyday language of the people instead of in classical Chinese that could be understood only by intellectuals. Like Mao, Lu Xun always understood his audience. His introduction to a short story collection titled *Call to Arms* (*Na Han*) sent a profound message to me:

> When I was young I too had many dreams. Most of them I later forgot, but I see nothing in this to regret. For although recalling the past may bring happiness, at times it cannot but bring loneliness, and what is the point of clinging in spirit to lonely bygone days? However, my trouble is that I cannot forget completely, and these stories stem from those things which I have been unable to forget.[1]

I always felt at ease with the ordinary working-class people in China. They would invite me into their homes, and we would joke and laugh together. We'd talk about everyday life, and I'd play with their kids. I became part of their families, and I could completely relax. I did not hang around with intellectuals. I was never an intellectual, and I still do not consider myself one. I have always thought of myself as a working-class person. The workers were straightforward and honest in what they said, unlike the intellectuals and bureaucrats, who always said what the government wanted them to say. When they talked to me, it was usually the company line. When the workers talked to me, it was about life. These people taught me the simplicity of living rather than its complexities. I had been given the opportunity to be exposed to a little more education than most of them, but that did not mean I was in any way a better human being. I was just an ordinary person who had learned a few things. So it was natural for me to sit down and talk with these people. It was not something I had to learn; in truth, it was all I knew how to do.

I became especially good friends with the cooks in the cafeteria at Wuhan University. They would cook something, and then we'd sit down and eat, drink, and tell jokes. We'd eat plain, earthy food such as chicken feet or pig intestines and drink a powerful Chinese rice liquor called bai jui that was so strong you could light it with a match. Oh, they were big drinkers, and I had a great time with them. When I was not studying, that's where I was.

In 1957 I volunteered to join other Chinese students and go to the countryside to help build a railroad. Students from different departments and various universities tried to outdo each other, and I really enjoyed this fierce competition. My group worked in a low area, so we had to build up the roadbed before tracks could be laid. First we dug up dirt; then we carried it in baskets, dumped it, and returned to fill another basket. The higher the roadbed got, the more difficult our work became. I ended up carrying a lot of dirt. I took off my long underwear and tied knots in the legs so I could fill both legs with dirt. Then I put the two legs around my neck. I looked really funny, with those legs hanging almost to the ground, but I was able to carry a lot of dirt. This freed my hands so I could also help carry baskets of dirt. Two of us would put a bamboo pole on our shoulders, with a basket on each end. We had to trot, and the trick was carrying this pole in such a way that the load went up and down rather than swinging from side to side; otherwise, it could trip you up.

I really enjoyed physical labor, and when it came time to eat, I'd eat a washbasin full of grain. We slept on boards in tents located a couple of miles from where we worked. It would take us thirty-five or forty minutes to walk to work in the morning, but considerably longer to walk back in the evening because we were so tired. We'd sing on the way home, and at night before we went to sleep, we'd put on little shows for ourselves and sing more songs. Because

I had volunteered, the Chinese students felt I was really one of them, and I enjoyed proving that I was. I was stronger than most of the other students, and I enjoyed showing just how strong I was. I guess all my life I've been a bit of a showoff.

I worked maybe a little more than a week on that railroad bed before the school insisted I return to my classes. I wanted to stay on, but school officials thought it looked bad to have foreigners doing this kind of work. I even went to the class leader and told him I wanted to stay, but he told me that the authorities had already decided that I had to return to school.

I always got along with my fellow students in Wuhan and made lots of good friends. We would talk, sing songs, exercise, and take walks together. Chinese students almost always go out in groups, and they would invite me to go with them. These relationships were very different from those usually found in America, where we stress individualism. Americans seldom do anything collectively, but in China we were never alone.

I liked to sing, and I learned many Chinese songs. I was also a good dancer and always tried to be in an upbeat mood. I had a loud laugh that could be heard wherever I went. I did not meet any students who were unfriendly, which certainly helped my adjustment. It is difficult to explain that atmosphere. After all, I had recently been an American soldier shooting at them, but now I was a fellow student, and they accepted me.

I also enjoyed participating in sports while I was in Wuhan. The average student at the university was seldom involved in sports, but sports had been my whole life. I played basketball, swam, ran track, pole-vaulted, and even got some of the students to play softball.

I even became very proficient at Ping-Pong. In fact, after I returned to Memphis, no one could beat me. I'd play for ten, twenty, or even fifty dollars a game. Guys came from everywhere to play me, but they found out they could not win. I used to go down to the police station and play the cops, but they told me I was hustling and not to come by anymore.

I played Zhuang Zedong an exhibition Ping-Pong match in Wuhan the same year he won the world championship. I got only three points, but that was very good against him. I suppose he did not have to let me get those three points, but maybe because I was a foreigner he felt sorry for me. I don't know for sure, but I like to believe that I earned them. I had a nice little slam, a good backhand, and four or five different serves. I could make the ball do some crazy stuff. But his ball was so fast you could hardly see it. By the time you got ready to hit it, it was already past you. He had serves that you had no idea what

Clarence Adams playing softball.

they were going to do after they hit the table. The best players in the world then were from China, Japan, and Korea.

· · · · · ★ · · · · ·

Initially, I also got along well with my professors and various university officials at Wuhan. They invited me into their homes and took me to movies and plays, but then something happened that changed their perception of me.

I did have a temper, and I did not like people messing with me, especially if I considered their actions to be racially motivated. I would react, perhaps too aggressively; at least, that's what several Chinese officials told me. They said I was too sensitive. They might have been right, because I know I can be difficult. If someone steps on me, I fight back. The first time this happened in China occurred shortly after we were allowed to leave our compound in Taiyuan. Morris Wills, Lowell Skinner, Albert Belhomme, and I went into town. All of a sudden, this Chinese peasant ran up and kicked me in the butt. When we got back to the compound, I asked a Chinese official, "Hey, you told me discrimination did not exist here. Why did this happen? Wills, Skinner, and Belhomme are big white guys. I was the smallest guy there, and the only one who was black, so why didn't he kick all of us?"

He explained that this peasant had just got out of some kind of mental institution. At least, that's what he told me. He said, "He didn't kick you because you are black but because he is crazy."

I told him, "Yeah, he was one crazy guy." That's when I was first told I was too sensitive.

The second incident occurred when I was waiting for a bus in Wuhan. A young peasant walked up to me and very loudly said something like, "Wow! Look at how black this man is! All the soap and water in the world couldn't wash him clean!" He did not know that I understood what he was saying. Then he became more agitated and said, "Look at his hair! It looks like burnt charcoal!" I still did not change my expression, pretending that I had not understood him. A crowd began to gather. The peasant then dared his friends to touch my hair. He kept right on talking and inching his way toward my backside. By then I was angry. Just as his fingers were about to touch my hair, I suddenly turned around and hit him right on the chin and knocked him down. My reflexes just took over, and I hit him. When I later thought about it, I realized he was probably an illiterate peasant who had never seen a black person and just wanted to have some fun. I do not think he meant any real harm, but at the time I just reacted.

A policeman came over and told the peasant, "Hey, you don't treat our foreign guests that way." Then other people also began criticizing him. When the bus came to take me back to Wuhan, the police put me on it alone. They did not want any more problems. By the time I got back to school, everyone already knew about me knocking this guy to the ground.

The dean called me into his office and told me, "You are a guest in China, and you should respect our people and their culture." Much later I figured out that he was probably referring back to when China was ruled by foreigners, who could do anything they wanted to the Chinese people, including hitting them. I apologized and admitted I understood that the guy really meant no harm and was just having fun at my expense. I tried to explain to the dean that it was simply a reflexive action, that it was Skippy, the angry seventeen-year-old Memphis boy, who had done it. For those who have never had to use violence to defend themselves, this probably sounded like a poor excuse, and certainly the dean did not seem to understand what I was trying to tell him. Without saying another word, I left his office.

After this incident I noticed that some of the professors and administrators changed their attitude toward me. These same individuals who had invited me into their homes or out for tea now built an invisible wall between us. This made me realize that deep down inside I would always be that tough kid from the streets of Memphis who could never become a passive intellectual, even with a million years of higher education.

These unfortunate experiences took me back to my early childhood. Growing up, I had always resented having to pretend to be nice to white people, although this was something every black child in the South had drummed into him at a very early age. We always had to show deference toward white folks. On the streets, we had to get out of their way or bow our heads, and when any white person talked to us, we had to answer "yes, sir" or "yes, ma'am."

I used to argue with my stepfather about this kind of humiliation. Sometimes our arguments turned so heated that he would whip me. I remember once when I was a young teenager he hit me so hard on the side of my head that I fell unconscious. When I came to, my mother did not even ask if I was all right. Instead, she acted like I deserved to be hit like that. I later understood what Fred was trying to teach me, and I was even able to apply his lessons when they might be to my benefit, like when I was working at the Peabody Hotel. But I always hated playing this role, and sometimes I just could not do it.

I especially resented having to act this way in front of white kids, and particularly if they were younger than I. I remember once when I was a teenager walking through a white neighborhood. It was summer, and white people were sitting on their front porches, chitchatting with their neighbors. All of a sudden, this little white kid came running up behind me, stuck out his tongue, and yelled, "Nigger, nigger, nigger!" I didn't like it, but I was afraid to do anything because I was in a white neighborhood. I tried to walk faster, but the faster I went, the faster this little kid ran behind me. He was still crying, "Nigger, nigger, nigger," and sticking out his tongue. All of a sudden, without even thinking about it, I turned around and grabbed his tongue and almost snatched it out of his mouth. I quickly turned it loose because it was so slimy, but by then he was lying on the sidewalk kicking and screaming, and all these white adults began chasing me. I was pretty fast for my age so I dodged into an alley and was able to lose them. It was a narrow escape and a dangerous adventure. Had they caught me, no telling what they would have done.

Strangely enough, a similar physical confrontation occurred the first time I really got to know my future wife, Lin. We had briefly met through some Korean exchange students I associated with, but that was about all. She had graduated the year before I arrived in Wuhan and was then teaching Russian at Wuhan Polytechnical University, which was adjacent to Wuhan University.

This fateful day the two of us just happened to be on the same bus in Hankou, which was the largest borough of Wuhan and located on the other side of the Yangtze River. The bus was so crowded I had to stand in the aisle. Sitting on one side of me was a lady holding a baby whose head was sticking out into the aisle. When the bus moved, I was careful not to lean into the baby.

This big Chinese guy, who I later learned was a student athlete used to getting special treatment, got on the bus and just bulled his way toward the rear, pushing people out of the way. When he pushed against me, I banged into the baby's head. Naturally, it began to cry, and the mother accused me of hitting her baby. So I grabbed this guy and we started shoving each other. I was stronger than he was, and I pushed him back through the standing passengers to the front of the bus. The bus driver opened the door, and I shoved him out. When he tried to get back on, the bus driver closed the door and drove off. Lin slouched down real small in her seat, pretending she didn't know me, and I pretended not to know her.

Other than these few incidents, I really had no problems with the Chinese people. And, of course, I would soon get to know Liu Lin Feng much, much better.

CHAPTER SEVEN

Marriage and Family

After I pushed that Chinese bully off the bus in Hankou, Lin and I went off to do our separate shopping. Later that same day when we again ran into each other, she asked if I knew my way back. I actually did, but I told her I had no idea how to find the bus stop. She told me, "Well, I will show you, but first I have to go home and pick up some things." Her family lived in a nice apartment in the center of Hankou. Her Aunt Yee Ma, who was actually a cousin to Lin's mother, and her younger brother Liu Li Quin lived there. Her older brother Liu Li Yueng also happened to be there that day. He was a college professor and a civil engineer. He and I immediately hit it off because we both shared the same passion for alcohol and laughter. I have always said, people who drink make better friends, and he was a heavy drinker. On many of my later visits, the two of us would take a washbasin to this little shop around the corner, get it filled with a rice whisky called *bai ju*, and then drink the whole thing. Unfortunately, the government never really trusted him because he was the eldest son of a well-known general and landowner, and he had also worked for Americans during the Chinese civil war. During the Cultural Revolution, the government sent him to the countryside and literally worked him to death. Lin also had an older sister, Liu Shu Sen, whose husband taught at Wuhan University, but I did not meet her until later.

Lin had lost both her parents when she was still a child, and she and her younger brother were raised by her older sister and Yee Ma, whose name literally translates as "Aunt Mother." Yee Ma would later help bring up our two children, as well as the children of Lin's younger brother.

When I first met Clarence Adams during his student days at Wuhan University, I liked him because he was a very strong person. He was very muscular and good in sports, but more important, he liked to study and wanted to acquire knowledge. He clearly wanted to improve himself. I also discovered that he was a very kind person, with a good heart, who treated the common people just like everybody else.
— Liu Lin Feng, wife of Clarence Adams

Lin's father, Liu Zuou Loon, had been one of China's most powerful warlords. In the 1930s he surrendered his army to Chiang Kai-shek, who was then in the process of defeating all the warlords and unifying China. Chiang Kai-shek made him governor of Hubei Province, the capital of which is Wuhan.

Like many powerful Chinese men of his time, Lin's father had two official wives plus several concubines. Lin's mother was his second wife. One of the sons from the general's first wife attended a very prestigious military academy in Japan, and the Japanese also used one of his mother's family residences as a headquarters during their occupation of China. Lin's mother's family, however, had been pro-American during World War II, and even after Mao and the Communists defeated Chiang Kai-shek in 1949, the pro-American side was initially spared because the United States had been China's ally during World War II.

During those chaotic years of World War II and the Chinese civil war, Lin never neglected her studies. In 1949 she entered Wuhan University, where she majored in Russian, after which she taught Russian at Wuhan Polytechnical University.

After that first memorable day with her family in Hankou, we started seeing more and more of each other. We'd take walks with the Korean students, and we gradually got to know each other. We were all older than the Chinese students, who were just coming out of high school and seemed almost like children to us. Some of the Koreans had been soldiers, even high-ranking officers. Their government had sent them to study and learn Chinese language, history, and culture, so they were very serious students. I got along with them because we were about the same age. We spoke Chinese to each other because they spoke no English. Their Chinese, of course, was much better than mine, but we could communicate. Some of them had lived near the Chinese border, so they spoke some Chinese even before they came to China.

They were mostly married, and I guess they thought I should be married as well. They told me, "We want you to meet someone, but she is not Korean. She is Chinese." They arranged for us to go to one of the parks with them. There was nothing about her becoming my girlfriend or anything like that. It was just to see how we mixed in with the group. The Koreans told me the next day, "She was impressed with you." So now it was up to me. I had to make the next move, just like in chess. I'm a pretty good chess player, so that day in Hankou was my next move.

I was very impressed with Lin. She was highly intelligent, and we talked about all kinds of things, even life in America. She was curious about the United States. I told her about my background, which of course was so very different from hers. She was shocked by my stories of racism and said she could not understand how human beings could do that to one another.

Several months after we started seeing each other, I was walking Lin back to her dormitory on a warm summer night, and I leaned over and stole a kiss on her cheek. She slapped my face and called me "thug," "hooligan," "imperialist running dog," and a few more choice Chinese words I did not quite understand. I was in a state of shock and thought she was crazy. We did not see each other for some time, but when we did, I apologized. She told me she forgave me, but only because I knew so little about Chinese culture. She informed me that the Chinese did not do such things. I still did not quite understand. Only much later did I find out that courtship in China was normally a much longer process, and that there was still a long way to go before I would be allowed to kiss her. I finally understood that I had jumped the gun. I also later learned that young lovers in China never show their emotions in public. In many cases we did not know who was dating whom until they announced their decision to get married.

Years later Lin explained to me that in spite of my kissing her, she already thought I was an open, friendly person with a good heart. I had forgotten the incident that had so impressed her, but she remembered that early in our friendship I had gone up to an old lady who was carrying a load of wood on her shoulder. I stopped, said hello, and took the wood off her shoulder and asked where she lived. She smiled, patted my shoulder, and told me. When we got to her house, her husband came out and shook hands and thanked me. Some of the neighbors stared at us. I guess they wondered, "What is this black man doing?"

After we became more serious, Lin and I often attended parties at the Hankou Hotel. It had been built in the 1920s by a German and was the best hotel in Wuhan. In the early 1950s the hotel was filled with hundreds of Russians who were helping the Chinese build a bridge across the mighty Yangtze River. Every weekend the hotel hosted a dance, and I was one of the regular guests, along with all these Russians.

Lin served as my Russian interpreter, so we fit right in. There was plenty of food, drink, and black caviar. I did not care much for those salty fish eggs or the black bread the Russians put them on, but I certainly enjoyed the free whisky and vodka.

The Russians loved to dance, and so did I. I had a good sense of rhythm, and very few partners could keep up with me. In all modesty, I thought I was a superstar on the dance floor. But this one night, when Lin and I were waltzing, a six-foot, three hundred–pound Russian woman cut in. In her massive arms, my head disappeared into her enormous bosom, and with my toes barely touching the floor, I looked like a black broomstick. We were supposed to be waltzing, but she dragged and slung me all over the place; in fact, she almost broke my back, tossing me around like a rag doll. When we finished, she told me that I really was a superb dancer. Then she went back and sat down with her husband. I sat down on the other side of the room, but she kept looking at me. I thought to myself, I hope she doesn't come over for another round. But when the band started playing a tango, she started grinning at me. I looked over at her husband, and he was smiling too. I guess he was happy she wanted to dance with me rather than with him. She started over toward me, but I sneaked off into the men's room and stayed there until the music stopped.

· · · · · ★ · · · · ·

After our courtship had gone on for more than a year, Lin and I decided to get married. Everyone in her family was very happy about the wedding except the brother of Lin's sister's husband, who was a dean at Wuhan University. He opposed the marriage, and did not attend the ceremony, although his wife gave us her approval. He was one of the few people in Wuhan who had a big, fine, Western-style home. He had studied at the University of Chicago in the 1940s and had accepted the prevailing white attitudes toward blacks. He told Lin, "If you really want to marry an American, at least marry a white man."

Lin's college, Wuhan Polytechnic University, also tried to give us trouble. When we went for our marriage license, we were told we had to have permission from her school. But some bureaucrat at her school told us, "We cannot grant you a license." I am not sure why, but earlier that year Lin had refused to volunteer to go to the countryside with me to work. When this same administrator had asked her why she refused, she told him she was planning to get married in a few months. He then asked, "What? You want to get married? Are you pregnant?"

That really made Lin angry and she told him, "No, we have not done that kind of thing. I know better than that. Our relationship is pure, but we like each other, and we are planning to get married before Christmas."

This same bureaucrat was now telling her she could not marry me. That made me so angry that I went to my guardians at the Red Cross and reminded them that they had promised me I could marry anyone who would have me. They quickly informed the administrators at Lin's school that they could not stand in our way.

We were married on December 20, 1957, but we did not marry the American way. We were not married in a church and wore no special wedding clothes. In reality, it was a reception, not a wedding. The university made a room avail-

Liu Lin Feng and Clarence Adams.

able for us, and we invited maybe fifty people. I was surprised when at least a hundred uninvited guests showed up. These were mostly peasants and workers who, along with the students, followed us to the reception hall, making jokes and wishing us well. Most of them had to stand outside looking through the windows during the ceremony, but the cooks from the cafeteria had fortunately prepared enough food for everybody, and we all had a great time.

After the reception, Lin and I made our way along a winding path leading to a guesthouse the university provided for our honeymoon. The foreign students had put wines, candies, and cigarettes in the guesthouse for us. Harold Webb and Richard Corden, two of the other former American POWs who were also studying at Wuhan, followed us into the guesthouse and made themselves at home. They drank up the wine and ate all the candy before I told them they had worn out their welcome and kicked them out.

After we got married, the authorities at Lin's school grudgingly gave us a place to live, but only after we again appealed to the Red Cross. Because some of its officials had opposed our marrying, they thought if we had no place to live, we could not marry. But Lin and I fought them until finally they gave in and provided us with a dark, dingy one-room apartment. Richard Corden came over and helped us paint, and Lin found some furniture and wall hangings, which transformed the room into a very warm, cozy living area.

A rumor, undoubtedly started by those same officials, had circulated around the university that Lin was already pregnant and that we had to get married. This made us so angry that we waited for several months before starting a family, just to prove that the rumor was a vicious lie.

When the peasants and workers heard the news that Lin was finally pregnant, they were curious about what the baby would look like. Some said the baby would have black and white stripes, like a zebra. Others thought the baby would be white on one side and black on the other, and there were even those who insisted the baby would look like a checkerboard with black and white squares. Needless to say, they were all waiting anxiously for the baby's arrival. Lin momentarily had her doubts as well, but I assured her that I had seen many mixed-blood babies when I was stationed in Japan and that they all had looked just fine.

Every day the old women at the market near where we lived would check Lin's stomach to make sure everything was okay and to decide whether it was going to be a boy or a girl. If her stomach was soft and came to a point, that meant a boy. If the stomach was flat, it was going to be a girl. They told us it was going to be a girl, and sure enough, our daughter, whom we named Di Lou after the mountain on which the university is situated, was born on January 3, 1959. We decided her English name should be simply Della.

Della became a beautiful baby, but she certainly was not pretty when I saw her right after she was born. Her face looked like one big blob: no nose, no mouth, no anything. I told Lin, "This cannot be our baby. She does not look right. Nobody will like her. Nobody will marry her, but I guess we'll just have to accept her as she is." I was really worried. The nurses tried to reassure me that everything was going to be all right, but I had never seen a newborn baby before. I went home and told Aunt Yee Ma, "I'm really scared. The baby is so ugly."

She told me, "Don't worry. You go back tomorrow, and you will see a different baby."

I could hardly wait for the next day to see what Della was going to look like. Well, she looked so different I could hardly believe it. The swelling had all disappeared, her color was normal, and I could see those big, beautiful, dark eyes. I was so relieved! All our peasant and working-class friends came to the hospital to see Della, and they were surprised to discover that she was all one color rather than whatever they had expected.

Della's birth was unfortunate only in the sense that 1959 was the first of three very difficult years for China. There was famine across the land, and we could

Baby Della at four months.

hardly get milk for Della. My school knew about our baby, so it sent me to this place in Wuhan where I could get powdered milk, but there was not even enough of that.

Food was so scarce because of Mao's disastrous Great Leap Forward. He was sure that collectivizing agriculture would produce a surplus of food, but it did not work out that way, and millions died of starvation. To make matters worse, the USSR was demanding that China repay its debt for the war materials the Soviets had furnished during the Korean War. It was my understanding that there had been some kind of agreement that China would furnish the manpower and Russia the equipment, but now the Soviets wanted their money, even though they were both fighting for the same cause. As a result, almost everything China produced went into paying this debt, and this naturally strained relationships between the two countries.

During these difficult years, friends were very important. I've already mentioned that I spent a lot of time with peasant farmers, street cleaners, clerks in the marketplace, and cooks in the university cafeteria. During tough times these people were always willing to help. I recall this one farmer who had practically nothing. I think maybe he had two hens. He needed everything he had for himself, but he came to our house very early one morning, before anyone was up, with an egg in his hand. He said simply, "I want the baby to have this egg for breakfast." Another time, a fisherman I did not even know brought over two fish he had caught that morning. He came to the door and said, "These are for the baby." I had no idea how to express my appreciation. When I tried to tell these generous souls I did not want to take their food because I knew their families needed it, Lin told me, "That is disrespectful. They have come all this way to give you this food, so you have to take it. If you do not, it will look like you think you are better than they are."

We took the fish and made a soup so it would go farther. We gave Della the flesh and we drank the soup. The school cafeteria did serve lots of vegetables, including many I had never eaten before. So we mostly ate vegetables and rice, and sometimes not very good rice. Occasionally we would be served some other kind of grain. Lin and I did not eat much. Della ate first, and what was left we got.

What do you say when people show you this kind of friendship? I was not used to anything like this in America. In China, if you make a friend, he is your friend for life. This is not always the case in America. As long as you are on top and doing well, you have got plenty of friends; but if you get in trouble and need help, you find out if they are real. This is how America was when I was growing up, and it is still this way. We are actually afraid of each other. We are afraid of saying too much to one another or getting too close. Americans may deny this, but that's simply what time it is.[1]

On August 4, 1964, our son Louis was born, and our Chinese American family was complete. This time no one made wild guesses about what our child was going to look like, because Della was already a beautiful child, and we had returned to Beijing and taken up residence in the international community, where one saw all kinds of nationalities. Aunt Yee Ma had accompanied us to Beijing to help care for Della, and now Louis would also receive her welcome attention.

Aunt Yee Ma holding baby Louis. Daughter Della is four.

CHAPTER EIGHT

The Foreign Languages Press, Africans, and the Vietnam Broadcasts

I graduated from Wuhan University in 1961 with my bachelor's degree in Chinese language and literature. The university threw a farewell party for us, and everybody had to make a speech, including me. Some official asked me to comment on my university experience. I said it was a great university, but that there is always the bad with the good. I told them that, generally speaking, I did not like the intellectuals because I did not think they were candid or completely honest. I said I enjoyed being with the common people who worked for the university, but not with those in the upper echelons.

Lin did not like what I said, but I had to be honest. After all, I had learned about self-criticism when I was a POW, and I meant my comments to be constructive. I told them they needed to know this for any future foreigners who might come to study. When I offered my criticism, they did not appear to be angry with me.

Of the nine former American POWs who attended a university, five of us completed our studies. Morris Wills and William White had remained at the People's University in Beijing and graduated; Harold Webb and Richard Corden completed their studies with me in Wuhan. The others went home or dropped out. William Cowart, Lewis Griggs, and Otho Bell left in the summer of 1955. By the end of 1958, Richard Corden and several others, including Lowell Skinner, had also returned to the States. I guess Skinner was disappointed after discovering he was not going to become a general. Harold Webb married a Polish girl he met in Wuhan and moved to Poland, and John Dunn moved to Czechoslovakia with his Czech wife. Scott

> *Growing up, I had a very negative impression of Africans. . . . We were told that Africans were savages who ran around in grass skirts, lived in jungle huts, and were cannibals. Worst of all were the Tarzan movies, with the great white ape-man. . . . But in Beijing the African diplomats accepted me with open arms, and I discovered they were a lot smarter than I and ten times better educated.*
> —Clarence Adams

> *The U.S. Army called me the new Tokyo Rose when I made those broadcasts directed at the black soldiers in Vietnam. That's why they hated me so much. . . . They did not want blacks to have a brain. The army made it clear: "We don't pay you to think. Just obey."*
> —Clarence Adams

Rush, Morris Wills, and William White married Chinese women and brought them back to America when they returned. James Veneris and Howard Adams also married Chinese women but remained in China.[1]

The Chinese sent me to Beijing after my graduation. I had no choice in the matter, but I was very happy to return to Beijing because it was a great metropolitan city. In Wuhan I was pretty much cut off and isolated from the outside world, but in Beijing I could find out what was happening outside of China.

By this time my command of the language was good enough to do simple translations. I had also developed an interest in classical Chinese novels, as well as the more modern writers like Lu Xun, so I was delighted when I was given a job at the Beijing Foreign Languages Press. William White and Morris Wills were also assigned to the Foreign Languages Press as translators.

Lin was not able to get a teaching position in Beijing because the government officials were suspicious of her. I am not sure why. Perhaps because of her family background or the problems we had with her university, they thought she might be a bad influence on her students. Whatever the reason, we later learned that government officials had warned some of our friends to stay away from us because they did not consider Lin to be completely trustworthy. Of course, no one ever came out and said, "We do not want you to work." They would make excuses like, "We can't find anything for you," which was not true, because other colleagues were getting positions. According to its own policies, the government had to provide a job for her, so it paid her sixty yuan a month not to work.

As one of China's leading publishers, the Foreign Languages Press's enormous staff turned out hundreds of books each year in more than fifteen foreign languages. In addition to various propaganda publications, the press produced translations of Chinese literary classics, children's stories, and art books. It also published a dozen or so prestigious periodicals. Naturally, I felt very proud that first day when I walked into my spacious and well-lit office in the English Language Department as a translator of Chinese children's stories and working-class publications.

At the time, the Chinese government was devoting a lot of attention to workers and peasants because they were the most progressive and reliable people in the country. After I became more proficient in Chinese, I took great satisfaction in helping edit some of the books we published for those who had little or no formal education. These were very small books, maybe five inches by three inches. They were simplistic, and always contained a Communist message, but they greatly helped the peasants and workers learn to read.

The government also wanted to show how creative the common people could be, so it promoted their writings. Many of these translations were down-to-earth stories about the lives of ordinary people. I found this kind of literature very appealing, and the better I got at translating, the more interesting they became. Because you could not simply translate word by word, I also learned to be innovative. People in various countries view things differently. For instance, in America we talk about the man in the moon, but in China it's a tree in the moon.

· · · · · ★ · · · · ·

I met a lot of foreigners during those early days in Beijing. Most were working in China as experts in one field or another, but others were visitors. One unforgettable day I had the good fortune to meet Dr. W. E. B. Du Bois and his wife, Shirley Graham, who were visiting China. At the time, Du Bois was America's most famous black scholar and author and was respected not only among African Americans but among all Africans and even many whites the world over. I had read some of his work in the prison camp, and I especially remember him saying, "The problem for twentieth-century America is the problem of the color line." Events certainly proved him correct.

Naturally, the foreigners I got to know best worked at the Foreign Languages Press. There were Americans, Swedes, British, and other Asians. I had a lot of contact with Betty Chang and Gladys Young, two Americans who had worked as translators for years. Gladys was married to Young Shiang Yee, and together they translated one of China's most famous pieces of eighteenth-century literature, Cao Xueqin's Hong Lou Meng (A Dream of Red Mansions). Both of them had high positions in the party and in Chinese society, but their son died during the Cultural Revolution, after being jailed and tortured.

Betty Chang, who had an American college degree, married a Chinese doctor. They had five children, all of whom now live in the United States, although Betty remains in China. Betty helped me a lot when I was starting out at the Foreign Languages Press, and she became very close to my family. Her son Bobby also became a childhood friend of Della's.

I had only limited contact with the other Americans at the Foreign Languages Press. Israel Epstein and Sidney Rittenberg had worked there for years. Their ties to the Chinese Communists went all the way back to the revolution, and they were now Chinese citizens. I was just learning, and the others were vastly superior at both translating and polishing their English translations. I was at the bottom of the rung. Even White and Wills had at least graduated high school, but I was just a high school dropout trying to make my way.

My salary at the Foreign Languages Press was enough to cover all our expenses. I received 250 yuan a month, which was a very good wage in China. For example, the average worker made maybe 60 yuan, and a professor between 100 and 200. We lived inside a walled compound with many other foreigners and several important Chinese families. Our housing was free and so were our medical expenses and even my whisky. All I needed money for was buying food and clothing.

After Louis was born, we moved into a large two-bedroom apartment, complete with a shower, telephone, and a large kitchen with a refrigerator. Neither Lin nor I had ever lived in a house with a refrigerator. We had a regular maid who did the cleaning and another one who did the laundry. There was a professional chef available for those of us living in the compound. He would cook Chinese or Western dishes, so Lin never had to cook unless she wanted to. We also had access to a limo service when we wanted to go out.

Beijing was a wonderful place for Della. She was able to attend a special kindergarten. Although she was the only child in the class who was not full-blooded Chinese, there was never any hostility directed toward her, either by the other students or the teacher. There were, in fact, several mixed-racial families living in our compound, but race was never an issue. Della later told me that not until we moved back to America did she become aware of racial issues. In China she never questioned who she was or who the other children were. Of course, there was a rude awakening waiting for her when we moved back to Memphis.

It was a carefree, relaxing life for all of us. Della had lots of children to play with inside our compound, but she wondered why she was not allowed to play with children who lived outside its walls. One day she sneaked out through a hole in the gate and made friends with a little girl who took her to a dark, dingy one-room apartment where she lived with her parents and some older person. The only bathroom was down the hall, which they had to share with other families. When the mother saw Della, she screamed at her to get out. Della ran home crying. Lin tried to explain to her that the mother was embarrassed and did not want her daughter to see what she could not have.

I loved to go to the Wan Fu King Market in Beijing. There were so many interesting things to see and fascinating places to eat. Another wonderful place was E. I. Ho Yuan, which was the Summer Palace. We could row a boat, take lovely walks, or just relax sitting on the grass. Nice, clean, wholesome fun. Tiananmen Square, which is the world's largest public square, also had lots to see. On the north side is the Gate of Heavenly Peace, and beyond it lies the Forbidden City. On the west side is the Great Hall of the People, and in the middle is the Monument to the People's Heroes. Hundreds of thousands of Chinese fill Tiananmen Square to celebrate public holidays and parades. Most Americans first heard about Tiananmen Square in 1989, when some two thousand students lost their lives for demonstrating against the Chinese government, but there were also demonstrations while I was in Beijing, including one that got me in trouble with the authorities.

····· ★ ·····

Our social life was limited in Beijing. In Wuhan we had been invited into a lot of Chinese homes, but among the higher officials in Beijing, things like that did not happen. Mr. Wong was the only official at the Foreign Languages Press to invite Lin and me to have dinner with his family. I never forgot that. It was such a good feeling to be invited into his home. We did socialize with Gladys Young and Betty Chang and their Chinese husbands, and we were very close to Morris Wills and William White, both of whom lived with their Chinese wives inside our compound. Their wives and Lin were the best of friends. We had little to do with Israel Epstein and Sidney Wittenberg, although both were Americans. They were so high up in the Foreign Languages Press that they apparently preferred to mix with people on that social level.

Among the foreigners in Beijing, it was especially the African diplomats who accepted me with open arms, and I came to spend more and more of my free time at their embassies. I made a special effort to become acquainted with the representatives of Ghana, Guinea, and Mali, the three African embassies then in China, but I also established good relations with the Cuban embassy.

I was especially curious to see what Africans were like. After all, I had never spoken to or even seen an African. The first embassy I visited was the Ghanaian, and I will never forget it. I knocked on the door, and a very heavy, coarse voice inside asked, "Who is it?"

I said, "It's me, Adams."

He said, "Who is Adams?"

I said, "I'm just an American."

"Oh, an American, huh? Well, come on in."

The Ghanaian first and third secretaries and a commercial attaché were drinking Johnnie Walker Black. The first thing they asked me was, "Do you drink?" I told them that I did. I had drunk American or Canadian whisky, but I had never had Scotch. There were three fifths of Scotch on the table, one for each of them. I reached for one of the bottles, but the third secretary said, "No, these are ours. We will get you your own bottle." He opened a new bottle for me and poured a water glass full and said, "Here, drink this. We will see if you are a man."

I put the glass to my lips and took a sip and started to set it down. The third secretary said, "No, no! Are you a man or what? You must drink it all!"

So I drank it down. I felt a burning sensation all the way down to my stomach, and tears began pouring down my cheeks. They laughed and said, "You're a man all right."

I thought, Well, I'm happy to learn that I'm a man.

They wanted to know why I had come to China and if someone had sent me to the embassy. I told them that no one had sent me, that I just wanted to meet some Africans. The first secretary was sitting there saying nothing, and I began to wonder why he was so silent. He was just watching me. Finally, the third secretary laughed and said, "You know, because you are a black American, you would make a very good agent to spy on us Africans."

I laughed and told them, "Oh, no, I'm too dumb to be a spy." I was afraid I might not get out of there alive if they thought I was there to spy on them. But they all laughed, and the first secretary said, "We don't trust American Negroes, especially the intellectuals. The American government sends Negroes to Africa to spy on us because the whites cannot find out anything."

I told him, "Hey, I'm not an intellectual. I come from a very poor family. We have nothing."

After that we all laughed and one of them said, "Now that you've drunk your whole glass, we can become sociable drinkers."

So I sat there enjoying myself. I drank that whole bottle they gave me, and I took two more home. That was the beginning. They told me that in the future I would always be welcome at the Ghanaian embassy.

Growing up, I had a very negative impression of Africans. White America had distorted our minds about such things. We were told that Africans were savages who ran around in grass skirts, lived in jungle huts, and were cannibals. Worst of all were the Tarzan movies, with the great white ape-man. Tarzan was so bad he could go into an African village and totally frighten all the inhabitants. They would be screaming and hollering and trying to run away. I was just a dumb kid. I didn't know any better. I thought, Hey, Tarzan ought to kill all of them. I was cheering for the great white man. Every black kid thought like that.

No one ever told us about the magnificent African kingdoms of antiquity or that Africans had highly developed civilizations long before the Europeans did. We were never taught about the extraordinary universities of ancient Africa, and we had no idea there were modern African cities. These negative images poisoned our minds. In fact, we were also never taught about great African Americans. We only learned about great white men. Our American history was one enormous lie. Whites wrote the books to reflect their own greatness and no one else's. They were always the creators and inventors. But we also invented and created a lot of things, but no one ever gave us credit.

So I was very impressed when I met genuine Africans. They were so intelligent. As I sat there, I thought, these people are a lot smarter than I am and ten times better educated. I was the little one, the one who needed to learn, and I realized that I could learn from them.

When I was finally introduced to the Ghanaian ambassador, he said to me, "Do not feel so great about your country. You do not even have a flag. We may be poor in Ghana, but we have our own flag, and we're our own boss. What do you Negroes have? All the stars in your flag are white." Then he said, "We Africans have driven out the British, French, Dutch, and German imperialists. We may not have much economic wealth, but at least we control ourselves, and that is very important!"

He was right. I certainly could not say that the Stars and Stripes in any way represented me. I may not have been conscious of it at the time, but his concept of being one's own boss would later become a guiding principle in my life. Very few blacks in the America of my youth ever considered not working for someone else. This was simply an alien concept, but it was precisely what later motivated Lin and me to open up our first Chop Suey House in Memphis. Friends would visit us and comment on the menial labor the two of us had to perform. When they asked why an educated man would want to do something like this, I always told them the same thing: "I would rather do hard, dirty work for little money than to be at the mercy of another human being."

I eventually became a trusted friend at the Ghanaian embassy. I even served as an unofficial adviser. The Ghanaians would invite me to sit in on official meetings with the Chinese and then ask me for my interpretation of what the Chinese had said. For example, did I think the Chinese were sincere in their remarks, and did they have any intention of actually doing what they said?

I received no money for doing this, but when I asked for something, I got it. For example, when the embassy sent someone to Hong Kong, I'd ask him to pick up some Johnnie Walker Black Label scotch, Gordon's Dry Gin, and vermouth. And if I wanted some new Western-style clothes, I would tell him my size, and they would be made for me in Hong Kong. I became especially close to Ampoufou, who was the Ghanaian first secretary. He came from a wealthy family that owned a great deal of land and lots of goats. His father was head of a clan and had, I think, four wives. Ampoufou once said to me, "If a man has a sufficient number of goats, he can have as many wives as he wants; he just has to be able to feed them." Then, he told me, "You bargain for

Clarence Adams dancing at the Ghana embassy with the daughter of the Cuban ambassador.

Clarence Adams (second from right) and African diplomats and wives at a Ghana embassy party. Adams's friend Ampoufou is fifth from the left; his wife is to his immediate left.

wives with goats, and sometimes you offer as few as possible to a father for his daughter. If you can get her for one goat, all well and good."

Like most Africans whose fathers were prominent landowners or heads of clans, Ampoufou had been well educated abroad, but he was also very outspoken and always said whatever came into his mind. Lin did not like him, but I thought he was very friendly and outgoing. He was a great jokester. He would grab Lin because she was so small and fling her around just like that big Russian woman had done with me. Lin said I should not trust him because he was too cunning and devious, but I never found this to be true, and we always had a good time together.

We probably did too much drinking together, and Lin did not like this. Sometimes she would go to the embassy parties with me, but I often went alone. Then, when I had too much to drink, I would come home very late and we'd get into arguments. Ampoufou would make fun of me when I told him Lin thought I drank and partied too much. He told me, "You think that you are no longer a slave because you have been emancipated, but you are still a slave to your wife, and this means you are still not a true man." I undoubtedly listened too much to him because this kind of thinking led to even more arguments with Lin. But in truth, Lin was every bit as strong an individual as Ampoufou, and I finally came to realize that her character and principles were much more admirable than his. Some of the Chinese officials had also become concerned that I was partying too much with the Africans.

When I was thinking about leaving China, Ampoufou was the first to offer his help. He told me I could get Ghana citizenship papers at his embassy, and that the Ghanaian government would set me up at the University of Accra, where I could teach Chinese. I thought about it, but I told him, "No, if I go anywhere, I might as well go back to America."

I also visited the Ceylon and Indian embassies, but I did not get as close to them because there was more of a cultural barrier and sometimes also language problems. I was always afraid of the British chargés d'affaires in Beijing. The Chinese had warned me that the British were very cunning and shrewd and that all were spies. The Americans were much more naïve than the British. The British had considerably more experience deceiving people than did the Americans, so I had to be especially cautious around them.

Through attending parties at these various embassies and my work at the Foreign Languages Press, I also had the privilege of seeing, and even meeting, some of China's most famous leaders, including Mao Zedong and Premier Chou En-lai. In the spring of 1963 the Foreign Languages Press was celebrating the fifth anniversary of one of its magazines, and Premier Chou En-lai was the guest of honor. Morris Wills, William White, and I were invited, and the premier took the time to sit down at our table and talk with us, as he did with everyone at the reception. He wanted to know if the three of us were happy with our lives in China, and whether there were any problems he could help solve. He seemed to have total recall of the precise details of everything that had happened to China, and even to us personally, and he shared his great knowledge with us. This made the three of us feel almost as important as the old-time foreigners in China, such as Epstein and Rittenberg.

In August 1965 I did something that greatly affected my situation after I returned to the States. Because of my position at the Foreign Languages Press and my foreign contacts, I had access to Western news publications such as *Time, Life,* and *Newsweek.* I read about the progress of the civil rights movement with great excitement and anticipation. I knew that if I had been home, I would have been right in the middle of the movement, and this also affected my decision to return home. The passage of the 1964 Civil Rights Act meant that my family could possibly have a life in America. Certainly, before the pas-

Clarence Adams (back to camera), Morris Wills (to Adams's immediate right), William White (facing Adams), and other Foreign Languages Press employees talking with Premier Chou En-lai.

sage of such laws, taking my interracial family to the South was out of the question. Now there was a degree of hope. But there was something else in these periodicals of even more immediate concern, and that was America's escalating war in Vietnam.

What was happening in Vietnam was all too familiar to me. The United States was fighting another war against communism in the name of freedom and democracy. I knew that once again many poor blacks would be sent to a remote foreign land to be slaughtered, just as I was. I wanted them to know what other young black Americans and I had gone through in Korea, and I soon had the opportunity to tell them.

I went to the Beijing office of the Vietnam National Liberation Front and volunteered to make a tape recording about my experiences in Korea. The resultant broadcast was certainly the most controversial thing I did in China, at least as far as the American authorities were concerned. I did not make a draft of my remarks, and I needed no rehearsal. In one breath I made a recording so powerful that everyone in the recording room was stunned. I do not remember everything I said, but I know I began by giving my name, rank, and army serial number. Then I said, "I am not broadcasting to the entire U.S. Army, only to its black soldiers." I went on to describe how my all-black regiment had been sacrificed to save white units. I asked the black troops one overriding question: "You are supposedly fighting for the freedom of the Vietnamese, but what kind of freedom do you have at home, sitting in the back of the bus, being barred from restaurants, stores, and certain neighborhoods, and being denied the right to vote?" I ended my remarks by urging them to "go home and fight for equality in America."[2]

My broadcast was aired through Radio Hanoi and broadcast to the American soldiers on the front lines over loudspeakers. The army, of course, monitored these broadcasts and labeled me the new Tokyo Rose. In the army's mind, a black man was not supposed to have a brain: "We don't pay you to think. Just obey" was the army motto. I never denied making these tapes, and the House Un-American Activities Committee cited them when it accused me of having "disrupted the morale of the American fighting forces in Vietnam and incited revolution back in the United States."

There were black soldiers from Memphis who heard my broadcasts. Years later, some of them came into the restaurant Lin and I owned and said, "Hey, you're the guy who made those broadcasts." They told me the army discussed them in its political indoctrination sessions with the soldiers. The army was apparently worried. Imagine what might have happened if black soldiers on the front lines had acted on my words.

Over the years, many people have asked me how I could have made those broadcasts and then decide to return to America. My answer is always the same: This is my country. I have as many rights as anyone. After all, we are all outsiders. The only indigenous people on the continent are the American Indians. They might be entitled to special rights. But the rest of us are just guests.

CHAPTER NINE

Going Home!

There were many reasons why I decided to go home.[1] I had no contact with people in America, except for an occasional letter, and I did get homesick. Because of the political friction between China and the U.S., I did not want to make things difficult for my mother and her family, so I never wrote about politics. They also did not write anything political. For example, we never mentioned race relations. We limited our letters to family news as a protection for both sides. My mother had already been diagnosed with serious health problems, and my sister Alice wrote me that if I wanted to see my mother while she was still alive, I should come home.

China was also beginning to wear on me. Even though the Chinese people always treated me well, I felt I had not made any contribution to their revolution, and I sometimes felt like a parasite. These people earned the right to have a good life, but I had not earned that right. I told someone, "I had to go to China for the right to create a good life, but I should have been able to do this in my own country."

There were other factors as well. The top Americans at the Foreign Languages Press, like Epstein and Rittenberg, were much better treated and respected than White, Wills, and I, in part because of their higher professional skills, and because they had taken part in the Chinese revolution going all the way back to the resistance against Japan during World War II. Because they were in the top positions, the three of us who had joined the Foreign Languages Press in 1961 realized we would never move up the ladder.

In August 1965 White, his wife, Hsieh Ping, and their two children left the press and went back to America.

I was in somebody else's country. I was enjoying my life, but I didn't earn it. Those people fought for what they had. It's theirs by right. I felt I was living off their country, and it got to be an embarrassment.
—Clarence Adams

U.S. and Red Cross officials waited at the bridge separating this British colony from Communist China for the return today of Korean War turncoat Clarence C. Adams. . . . Adams reportedly has made anti-American broadcasts for North Vietnam over Radio Hanoi.
—UPI wire service, May 9, 1966

He never told me why he was leaving. We did not consult with one another that much. Two months later Wills, his wife, Kai-yen, and their baby daughter left. I did not question him either. I just wished him well. Several of my other friends among the original twenty-one had earlier gone home, and now James Veneris and Howard Adams moved out of Beijing. That left me pretty much alone in the city. I could not really talk to either Epstein or Rittenberg, so if I wanted to talk to somebody who was not Chinese, I had to go to the embassies.

Foreigners were also coming under increased suspicion because of the Cultural Revolution, which began to surface in 1966. We did not know precisely what was going on, but we sensed there was trouble brewing for all foreigners. One could not wear Western clothes on the street without being attacked for capitalist ideas. We also noticed that certain friends and acquaintances became frightened to visit or even talk to us. Two of our friends were then suddenly deported, and this too brought us under suspicion.

I met John Horness, who was black, and his white girlfriend, Marga, at an embassy party. Both were British subjects. Marga was teaching English in a Chinese school, and John worked for the World Peace Committee in Beijing. John had a profound knowledge of Marxist political economy and international affairs, two of my favorite subjects, and we spent a lot of time together. Through John I met many of the African students who were studying at various universities in Beijing. On Sundays I would invite some of these students to our apartment, where John would lead discussions on politics, and I would supply whisky and some down-home Southern cooking.

Marga was fired from her school, but we did not know why. Then I heard rumors that John was a spy and that he and Marga had been ordered to leave the country. I certainly did not think he acted like a spy. I knew he loved good music and lively discussions, but I saw nothing else. I went to his house and asked him point-blank, "Are you a spy?" He admitted that he was, which truly shocked me. He never told me why he would want to spy on China. In spite of this, we remained friends, and I saw them off at the airport.

Not long after the expulsion of John and Marga, officials from the Chinese Red Cross questioned me about the Sunday meetings we hosted in our home for them and the African students. They wanted to know if there was any connection between what went on at these social gatherings and the several African student demonstrations in Tiananmen Square. I assured them that no such connection existed and that we were just getting together to discuss political economies.

The Red Cross also asked why I spent so much time at the African embas-

John Horness is wearing the hat; Marga is to his immediate left.
The others are mostly students.

sies. I am sure they knew about the good food, whisky, and clothes I had received, but with the Horness case in mind, they probably suspected me of spying for the Africans. They asked me, "What do you talk about when you visit these African embassies? Do you talk about China?" I was completely open in explaining our conversations: "Yes, we do talk about China, but I only tell them the things that I have seen with my own eyes. I do not look for negative things, but I cannot tell them that everything is beautiful. Sometimes I tell them about things that need improving, but I always emphasize positive things like the tremendous progress China has made and how much better off the people have become since the Communists took over and how bad things were under Chiang Kai-shek. And I always tell them how everybody now has plenty of food on their tables."

I told the Red Cross that the African diplomats wanted to know about the lives of ordinary Chinese. The diplomats knew how the top officials lived, but they did not know about the common people. Did they have enough to eat? Were they comfortable? When the Africans were unable to find this out for themselves, they asked me because I had so many contacts with ordinary Chinese. Once again, I told the Red Cross people precisely what I had told the Africans: "The Chinese people now have three good meals a day, although in the past many people did not know when their next meal was coming. And that is what life is about. You need a roof over your head, clothes on your back, and food on your table. The Chinese people under the Communists receive this." Of course I did not know any important Chinese secrets, but I did know something about the common people, and that is all I talked about with the Africans.

Shortly after this interrogation, the Red Cross suggested that I go to work in the textile mills in Jinan, the capital of Shandong Province, some three hundred miles south of Beijing. They told me the Foreign Languages Press no longer needed so many translators, which was certainly untrue, because Wills and White had already left for the U.S. I knew that to send a college-educated person to work in a factory was a form of punishment, so I refused to go. I told them I did not want to lose the cosmopolitan and international aspects of Beijing that I so enjoyed. In truth, I did not trust them, and I feared it might be dangerous for me if I no longer had access to my international contacts with the outside world. After refusing to go to Jinan, I had clearly worn out my welcome in Beijing.

· · · · · ★ · · · · ·

I began to focus more and more on certain negative aspects of Chinese life. These were not necessarily new to me, but they now really began to bother me. For example, I had never liked those Chinese officials and intellectuals who seldom divulged their personal opinions or inner thoughts and who always expressed only the official viewpoint. I now began to realize that there was also a lack of freedom of thought and speech in China.

When I discussed what was happening with Lin, she made it clear she did not want to leave, because she was afraid to go to the States. We had many heated arguments with lots of screaming and crying. Several times Lin agreed to go, but then she would change her mind. Finally, after Lin again tentatively agreed to go, I went directly to the Chinese Red Cross officials, without telling Lin, and told them we were leaving. When I came home and told her what I had done, she cried longer and harder than ever before. It was like her life had come to an end. Yee Ma was still living with us, and she was also in tears. After all, she had pretty much raised Lin and had also helped raise Della and Louis.

Lin's family also was not enthusiastic about her leaving. Before we left, Lin took Della and Louis to visit her family in Wuhan one last time. Every day they were there, Lin's sister tried to convince her not to leave China. She cried and yelled at Lin and said bad things about me. Years later, Della told me she did not understand all this. She thought her aunt was being crazy and mean, and she particularly resented what she said about me. At the time, I thought Lin's sister felt betrayed because I had promised never to go back to America, and she feared what might happen to Lin and the children in the States. She had heard stories about how badly some American men had treated their Asian wives once they were back home.

I could understand Lin's family's concern because we really did not know what would happen after we got back to Memphis. Only after we were back in Memphis did Lin explain to me that her sister had fussed and screamed at her and cursed me because she had to make a big show for the others living in the house, who always reported anything they heard to the authorities. The house had originally belonged to Lin's family, but the Communists had taken it over and allowed three other families to share the house with them. So in the hope of not suffering later retribution, Lin's sister had to sound like she was totally against us leaving.

Unfortunately, the act did not work, and government officials really went after Lin's family after we left. They removed almost everything from the family home, including furniture, jewelry, paintings, and priceless silk hangings. They even abused Aunt Yee Ma, who was then in her eighties, by taking her outside and cutting off her long braid. Finally, they forced Lin's younger brother to leave Wuhan and go to work in the countryside.

One encouraging note for Lin was that she had received letters from the Chinese wives of White and Wills telling her that life had greatly improved for blacks in America. White had found a job back home in Arkansas, and Wills also seemed to be doing all right, especially after he published a very critical article about his experiences in China in Look magazine shortly after his return. Lin naturally did not want to separate the children from me, and she also realized that if she and the children remained behind, they would always be under suspicion because of her associations with me and our friends.

When I told my friends at the Ghanaian embassy that I had definitely made up my mind to leave, they again offered to help me if I wanted to settle in Ghana. Once more I politely declined, because I knew that such a decision might be very dangerous for me. I did not fear the Ghanaians, but I certainly did the American government. Quasi-secret agencies like the CIA and the FBI could be very treacherous, and they really hated me. They wanted to try me for a variety of alleged crimes, including treason, because of those 1965 broadcasts I had made to the African American troops in Vietnam. If I had gone to Ghana, they might very well have sent someone to assassinate me. The question was whether the Ghanaians would have protected me, or would they have turned me over to the Americans? I did not know the answer, so I figured my best chance for survival was in my own country. At least if I disappeared in the United States, somebody would notice, but if something like this happened in an African country, no one would ever have known what had happened.

..... ★ .....

The Ghanaians told me that I had better leave as soon as possible, because there was growing political unrest in China that might endanger my family and me. They did not tell me any of the details, but they were, of course, referring to the Cultural Revolution that was then just beginning. They also suggested that because there was no American embassy in China, I should go to the office of the British chargé d'affaires, which was handling problems for Americans living in China.

In early May 1966 I told the British that we wanted to leave China. They immediately contacted the American consulate general in Hong Kong, and a few hours later all the major newspapers in Hong Kong and the United States announced that I was coming out from behind the Bamboo Curtain.

During the next couple of weeks we sold everything we owned. It broke Lin's heart, but we sold our beautiful ebony furniture and cabinets, our children's toys, and most of our clothes. All we took with us were a couple of dresses for Lin, a few outfits for the children, and two suits for me. Some of my relatives in Memphis sent us a couple thousand dollars for our passage, and we had almost three thousand dollars from the sale of our possessions and from money Lin had carefully saved.

We took a train to Canton, where we were met by Mr. Li of the Chinese Red Cross. He turned out to be a very nice young man, but he informed us that his superiors were very upset that I had not informed them earlier that we were leaving. He said I should have had enough trust to have allowed the Red Cross to notify the American embassy in Hong Kong that I wanted to leave. He was right, because it was stipulated in the armistice agreement that no matter what country we went to after leaving Korea, if we decided to leave, the government of that country would have to release us.

Mr. Li told us that high-ranking government officials were concerned about what I might say about China after I returned home. None of the other returning Americans had spoken favorably about their years in China; in fact, some had vehemently attacked China and its government. Morris Wills, for example, wrote some terrible things about China that certainly were not true. He later visited me in Memphis and told me I should have done the same thing because doing so would have made things easier for me after my return. Maybe he was right, because he was able to get a degree in library science and a good job as a librarian at a college in Utica, New York. But I could not do something like that. I sincerely believed that for the most part, China had treated me well.

I tried to reassure Mr. Li that I would never turn my back on China. I told him, "We are still friends, and we will always be friends. I have nothing but pleasant memories, and I am not going to attack you. I am leaving simply because I want to go home."

Mr. Li put us up in the White Cloud Hotel, which was the best hotel in Canton, and then showed us around the city and the surrounding countryside. He took us to a lot of beautiful places, and we ate in the best restaurants. Lin and the kids had a good time and temporarily stopped worrying about what lay ahead. This interlude lasted about a week, after which we boarded a train bound for Shenzhen, the border town across from Hong Kong.

On May 26, 1966, my family and I crossed the Luohu Bridge into Hong Kong. The bridge was only fifty meters long and manned by guards at both ends. At the Chinese end, an officer stamped my papers and said to me in English, "You can go now." Only then did I realize that once again I had embarked on a journey of no return. I was thirty-seven years old, and more than twelve years had passed since I first crossed the Yalu River into China. I thought to myself, I'm a changed man; nothing will ever again intimidate me. I picked up two-year-old Louis in my arms, and, holding seven-year-old Della by the hand, Lin and I walked slowly across the bridge. I did not look back.

Lin, however, kept staring back, and every time she did, she waved at Mr. Li, who stood quietly back on the mainland. Lin had become very fond of this kind and well-mannered young man. She undoubtedly realized that he would be the last of her countrymen she would know for a long time. Or perhaps he stood for all the relatives and friends she was afraid she would never see again. As she slowly walked farther and farther away, she could still see his lips moving, and she knew he was saying, "Take care. I wish you a safe journey." She could not hold back the tears.

As we stepped off the bridge into British Hong Kong, several American officials stood waiting. The American consul general stepped forward and greeted me: "Hello. I'm Nicholas Platt, and I'm glad to meet you." I shook his hand and stepped forward apprehensively, waiting for whatever was going to happen next.

Before we had a chance to go to our hotel or rest, I was ushered into a news conference at the Foreign Correspondents Club of Hong Kong. Immediately, someone asked me about my broadcasts to the black troops in Vietnam. I told the reporter that I had volunteered to make these broadcasts because I opposed the U.S. being in Vietnam and I wanted to encourage black soldiers to stop fighting. According to a wire service account, my precise words were, "The United States is involved in a war in Viet Nam that is not in the interest of the country. Negro soldiers are fighting for others when they themselves don't enjoy equality."[2] When another reporter asked me if I hoped the United States would win the war, I told him, "I hope to do something that will save more American lives." In response to another question I said, "The Chinese believe the United States may attack at any time. They're making all the preparations they can make."[3]

The next morning I was taken to the American embassy for what Consul General Platt called a "chat," but this chat lasted a week. Each day, waves of interrogators from different segments of the State Department questioned me. Each wanted to know a specific thing, and he would grill me on that topic. Then others would try to cross me up and make me contradict myself. They would twist and turn their questions around and then ask them all over again. It was stressful, but I was mentally prepared. I knew before I left China that I would have to go through something like this, and I had made up my mind that I was not going to lie about anything. I knew that if they caught me in a lie, they would work it over and over until they caught me trying to cover it up with more lies. So I was determined to say the same thing every time. Above all, I wanted to convince them that as a black man, everything I did was justified and within my rights.

They kept us in Hong Kong for almost three weeks, and we had to pay for our own hotel room. In addition to all the interrogations, I guess the American officials were still not sure they would allow us to go home. Finally, we cleared all the red tape and set sail for America via Honolulu on the luxury liner U.S.S. *President Cleveland.* Because Hong Kong had been so expensive for us, I purchased economy-class tickets, which meant the family would have to split up. Louis and I would be put in one stateroom and Lin and Della in another. But the government officials responsible for us paid the extra money to move us into second-class cabins because such an arrangement made it easier for them to keep an eye on the entire family. This move also made it easier for us, and the children had lots of fun watching movies, eating all kinds of good food, and making friends.

When the ship docked in Honolulu, we were able to go ashore. Once again, the children had a really good time. Della remembers going to a marine show with lots of dolphins and visiting her first Western-style store. She was fascinated by all the things she could buy there, and we did purchase some snacks to take back to the ship. Della was also happy to find another bottle of 7-Up, which she had first tasted in Hong Kong.

The Adams family in Honolulu.

Secret, unposed photos taken of the Adams family in their hotel in Honolulu.

The downside of Honolulu was that we again had to face the news media and additional interrogations by government representatives we had not seen before. On the ship they were probably from the CIA, but in Honolulu and San Francisco it was the FBI that took over. Government agents even took secret photos of us, which they later sent us. I guess they wanted us to understand that we would constantly be under surveillance.

I became very tired of the media harassing us everywhere we went. All I could see was flashbulbs going off. They simply could not get enough pictures of us. They were especially bad in Hong Kong, but they were also all over us in Honolulu and San Francisco. If we went out shopping, they were there taking pictures. They were everywhere in the hotel. I guess they were in a hurry to get pictures of me before I disappeared or was killed. I got so angry with a Japanese photographer in Hong Kong that I grabbed his camera and smashed it on the ground. I should not have done that, but when he insisted on sticking his camera right in our faces, the old anger flared up, and I reacted.

The passengers on the ship were very nice to us, at least until we landed in San Francisco on the Fourth of July, when some of them turned hostile. One of them yelled at me, "Hey, turncoat, why did you come back?" I guess he wanted to show the reporters who met the boat that he was a good American.

In San Francisco I again faced the usual battery of reporters. Their first question was always, "Why did you become a Communist?" I told them, "I never considered myself a Communist. I've always considered myself a loyal American. I never turned my back on my own country, and in that sense I'm not really a turncoat."[4]

We stayed in San Francisco for only a couple of days. An elderly and very polite FBI man named Bob made hotel arrangements for us. He also asked us where we wanted to settle in the United States. Without hesitation, I told him I wanted to return home to Memphis, but he warned me that the people in the South would not understand what I had done, which would certainly cause problems for my new family. He suggested I stay in a coastal city on the West Coast or the Northeast, where there was a greater variety of people and we could blend in with the crowd. He was certainly right about not being able to blend in with anyone in Memphis. Nevertheless, I told him, "I did not travel four thousand miles in order to hide. Memphis is my home, and that's where I want to go."

In reality, I wanted to return to Memphis because I understood it better than any other place, and of course my family lived there. I did not know anything about New York or San Francisco or any other American city, but I did know how to survive in Memphis.

CHAPTER TEN

Recriminations

The United States that Clarence Adams and his new family faced in 1966 was radically different from the one he had left in 1947 when he joined the army. The country was in the midst of the most turbulent decade in its history. It was fighting its longest and most controversial war in Vietnam, while at home it was embroiled in a civil rights movement that had become increasingly violent, with deadly riots breaking out in the Watts section of Los Angeles and in other cities across the land. Blacks, as well as other minorities and women, were becoming more and more impatient to gain their respective economic, social, and political rights. Then, two years after Adams returned to Memphis, Dr. Martin Luther King Jr. was assassinated in his hometown. Yet the decade held considerable hope for African Americans. The 1964, 1965, and 1968 Civil Rights Acts collectively prohibited discrimination in jobs and housing and the segregation of public accommodations while guaranteeing voting rights. But before Clarence Adams could enjoy any of these positive changes, he had to face a government that wanted to try him for treason.

It was a long train ride from San Francisco to Memphis. Della and Louis were once again very excited, constantly running back and forth through the cars. I just sat there, looking out the window, feeling increasingly apprehensive. Across from me sat a black soldier who recognized us from a newspaper photo. He had fought in Vietnam, and he told me he and his buddies had heard my broadcast telling them that they should not be fighting in Vietnam until they had won their human and civil rights back home. He agreed that racial tensions in Vietnam had been very bad, but after my broadcast, conditions had slowly improved. He described how black soldiers had previ-

> You only have one home, and mine is Memphis.
> —Clarence Adams, 1966

> I volunteered to fight for this country. I was not drafted. I spent three years in a prison camp and lost the toes on my right foot. I helped bury two thousand men in that POW camp, boys who wanted to live just like you and me. I went through all that hell, and Jimmy Carter is pardoning all these Vietnam draft dodgers and guys who refused to fight, but I cannot even get my back pay or my own money out of my military savings account.
> —Clarence Adams, 1977

ously pulled the most dangerous assignments, such as patrolling at night, but now white soldiers had begun patrolling with them. He also told me that the army had labeled me the black Tokyo Rose. When he got off the train, he shook my hand and said, "It's been nice meeting you, man. Good luck to all of you."

I outsmarted the news media and a large number of angry whites who were awaiting my arrival in Memphis. I had called my mother from San Francisco and told her I was coming by train and to meet me at the Grand Central Railroad Station on the afternoon of July 8. However, to throw off anyone who might be there to harass us, we arrived at one o'clock in the morning without notifying anybody except Uncle Peter, who picked us up at the station and quickly rushed us out the door. So when the reporters and angry white folks went down to the station that afternoon to confront us, we were already at my mother's house. The media people were so upset they called the house and angrily told me, "We wasted a lot of money sending out reporters and setting up our equipment and you didn't show up." I laughed and told them, "That's your problem."

I had developed this scheme while I was in our hotel in San Francisco. I remembered the children's story about the three little pigs and the big bad wolf. When they had to go and pick apples, the three little pigs told the wolf to meet them at six o'clock. They, however, went at five, so when the wolf arrived, they had already been there and picked their apples. And when the wolf figured out they were going at five, they fooled him again and went at four. So, like the three little pigs, I arrived several hours early in order to trick the wolves. I later heard from black friends who had gone down to meet us that there were lots of angry whites waiting for me.

I finally did grant the news media an audience. They came over and set up their cameras at my mother's house, and I gave them a long interview. They took some pictures, but they did not want to get too close to me after what I had done to that Japanese reporter in Hong Kong. I was still pretty belligerent and angry about a lot of things. I told them that I had not sold out any of my fellow prisoners and that I was not a turncoat, because under the terms of the armistice, I was a free man who was entitled to live wherever he wished. I said that China had been a great experience and that I had no regrets about going, because at the time I honestly believed China had more to offer me than my own country; after all, America's precious freedoms certainly did not exist in the Memphis of my youth. I did admit that I was pleased to see that there had been progress in race relations in Memphis and that I was very impressed that the "Whites Only" signs had disappeared from the train station.

The newspapers the next day reported some of what I told them but not all. Neither of Memphis's two white papers printed my explanation that I had gone to China because racism at home prevented me from having a decent life; nor did either mention that I had sneaked into Memphis early to avoid angry whites at the train station; and both papers always referred to me as "the turncoat." For example, on July 4, the *Press-Scimitar* announced, "Turncoat Lands in the United States." Four days later its headline was "Korean War Turncoat Due in Memphis Tonight." The *Commercial Appeal*'s banner challenged my veracity: " 'Loyal Citizen,' Turncoat Says." Memphis's black newspaper, the *Tri-State Defender*, avoided negative labels and recognized that I had also been a soldier. "Ex-GI Faces Problems of Supporting Family" was the page one headline of its July 16 edition. It also stated that I had "allegedly defected," and it was the only newspaper to acknowledge that I had been able to attend college for seven years in China and had personally met and talked with Chairman Mao and Chou En-lai.

Of course, I was also labeled a turncoat in the national press. Shortly after I arrived back in Memphis, nationally syndicated columnist Morris Ryskind lamented the fact that "[Adams has] come back to us on this very July 4, and hopes to teach at one of our universities. He'll probably make it, too. Maybe at one of those universities, which, in the name of academic freedom, would be willing to accept a Benedict Arnold Chair in History." [1]

The American Legion predictably also opposed my return. On June 7, Commander Cliff Hankel of American Legion Post no. 57 in Morristown, Tennessee, sent a letter to the state legislature saying, "The Volunteer State has never had a turncoat and doesn't want one now." [2] But a reader in the *Press-Scimitar*, who had a son in the military, defended me. Of course, she was black and understood why racism could be such a motivating factor:

> The night before my son was to be inducted into the army he was arrested for running a caution light. Before he was taken into the jail, the police punched him in the stomach, causing him to fall to the ground; then they kicked and cursed him. Why? Because he has been educated to answer questions with an intelligent "yes" or "no" rather than a "yassSUH" or "nawSUH." I am not a member of one of the so-called controversial groups. I am not a racist, an integrationist, or a radical. I am just a Negro, like so many others in the United States, who wants to be recognized as a human being. I do not know Clarence Adams, but feel it is safe to say he has the same feelings. [3]

For more than a week after we returned to Memphis we did not leave the house. We were getting lots of threatening calls from members of the Ku Klux Klan and other angry whites. They'd call us on the phone and say ugly things and threaten to burn down our house. At first we were naturally reluctant to leave the house, but then I decided I was not going to allow these people to stop me from living my life. I told Lin, "We're going out, and we'll see what they do." So Lin and I took the children to Katz's Drug Store, which was a pretty good walk from my mother's house on Doris Street. When we walked in, people immediately spotted us, and everything came to a halt. Nobody said anything to us, but I could hear the people whispering to each other, "Hey, that's him. That's him." All the people kept staring at us. At the time, I may well have been the only black man in Memphis, or the entire state of Tennessee, to have married outside his race. There we were, a black man, a Chinese woman, and two brown-skinned colored kids who looked neither black nor Asian. The Adams family must have looked like four Martians who had just walked in from the planet Neptune.

Then this one white fellow walked up, called me a turncoat, and spit at me. I started to grab him, but Lin stopped me and said in Chinese, "Ignore him. Remember, we've got the children with us." I stopped, and we continued walking around the store. At the soda fountain I bought drinks for Della and Louis. The cashier was a middle-aged white female. When she handed me my change, she said with a smile, "Welcome back to Memphis." I have never forgotten her and that warm smile.

I just wanted to prove I was not afraid to go out openly on the streets of Memphis. I think it worked. The threatening telephone calls continued, but no one lifted a finger to harm us. I could tell these calls were from whites by the voices, because blacks and whites do not sound the same. Some still insisted they were going to burn down our house. Others simply shouted into the phone, "Nigger, nigger, nigger" and, bam, they'd hang up. They said all kinds of nasty things to irritate us, and they really upset my mother; in fact, she increasingly blamed my return for all this trouble and embarrassment.

My mother had greeted me warmly when I first got back home because we had not seen each other for sixteen years, but even then it should have been a more joyous occasion than it was. There was a lot of silence, even on the part of my sisters. It was not the big, warm family reunion I expected after being away from home for such a long time, and I was very disappointed. I also wanted my family wholeheartedly to welcome my wife and children, but they did not. It greatly hurt me that Lin did not get the greeting she deserved, especially because her family had welcomed me with open arms. Lin could feel this, and although she initially said nothing, I could see the disappointment in her face.

My family also did not grab our kids and hug them like a family should. When I visit people who have small children, I always try to say something nice to the kids. They did not do that with Della and Louis, and this really hurt. Even before we left China, I had told a concerned Lin, "Don't worry, everything will be all right. If the rest of society doesn't welcome us, I still have a mother, sisters, aunts, and uncles who will provide a good support system." I convinced Lin that all would be well, and I actually thought it would be. But the family I found when I returned was not the same family I had left, which made it seem like I had lied to Lin.

Lin and the children simply did not understand this lack of acceptance. Part of the problem was that my sister Nellie and her two children were also living in my mother's two-bedroom house. This made things very crowded, but that was still no excuse for the way they treated Lin and the children. Years later, Nellie's daughter Carol and Della would become very good friends, but at the time Carol was only ten, and she was especially cruel to Della. She called her "Chink" and accused her of being dirty. She also would not allow Della to play with her friends. Once, when Della went to get some ice water from the refrigerator, Carol said to her, "You should always ask before you open the refrigerator. This is not your home, you know." Of course, Carol was too young to know any better, but my mother and sister observed this in silence, even after Della ran back to Lin in tears.

My mother was a good seamstress, and she enjoyed sewing clothes for Carol, but she never made any for Della, so this too made Della feel unwanted, and Lin felt the same way. One day my mother was making biscuits. She filled one tray with fresh dough and was about to fill a second tray. Lin, in the way a typical Chinese daughter-in-law would do, washed her hands carefully and was ready to help. She stood by Toosie for a while and watched her working. Out of curiosity, she gently touched the dough. "Stop that!" Toosie shouted. "I hate people to touch what I'm cooking!"

Lin jerked her hand away as if it had been burned by a hot iron, saying, "I only wanted to help."

"I don't know if your hands are clean," said Toosie.

"You saw me washing my hands!" Lin said loudly while running back to our room.

Even after years of reflection, I am still not sure why my family reacted this way. Perhaps I had deluded myself because I wanted so desperately to believe that my mother loved me, and of course, by extension, my wife and children as well. When I am honest with myself, I have to admit she had never been overly warm toward me, but it was very difficult for me to face up to this harsh reality.

Nellie later told me that our mother had gone through hell after I decided not to return home after the war. The FBI harassed her for years. They kept questioning her, talking with neighbors, and tapping her telephone. They made her feel that she had done something wrong in the way she raised me. She understandably resented this intrusion in her life, and my returning home must have made her fearful that this harassment and embarrassment would start all over again.

Another problem was that my mother wanted me to follow the example of Morris Wills, who had returned to the States the previous year. Wills wrote a long article for *Look* magazine for which he supposedly received $10,000. He said that life was terrible in China and that he now regretted his decision to go there. Then, shortly after I returned, Wills published his autobiography, *Turncoat*,[4] in which he went into even greater detail about how bad things were in Communist China. My mother and sisters hoped that I would do the same thing, not just for the money, which we all badly needed, but to redeem myself as Wills had done.

A couple of years later Wills and his family came to visit us in Memphis. When I asked him why he had written so negatively about his experiences in China, he said, "Now that you are in Rome again, you'd better act like a Roman." I disagreed and told him, "I am not going to bite the hand that fed and educated me and gave me a good job. You should also remember that both of us married Chinese women." Our families remained friends, but I could never agree with what he said about China.

Without question, I was singled out by the American government more than any of the other twenty-one who returned to the U.S. after 1955. For example, White and Wills had pretty much done everything I had in China, including participating in protest demonstrations in Beijing's Tiananmen Square against American foreign policies and the Vietnam War. White had also publicly demonstrated in support of the African students, but the government did not harass either of them to the extent it did me.

The U.S. Army had already court-martialed me for alleged violations of military law in the prisoner of war camp, although I was not there to defend myself. In addition, the government had compiled a several thousand–page file on me, including all kinds of accusations leveled against me by fellow prisoners after they returned home. If I had returned to America in 1953 with the rest of the POWs, I could have confronted my accusers and made them prove that I did all this. For example, I had supposedly informed on a fellow prisoner of war, and as a result, he was beaten. That was a total fabrication. A lot of witnesses also testified that I was reporting directly to the Chinese. I did go to the camp headquarters, but I was not reporting anything about the other prisoners. I was there to participate in study groups, where we learned about Maoism and Leninism. Some said I got special treatment, and maybe I did. Several of us also wrote articles for our camp paper, *Toward Truth and Peace.* When we did this, the Chinese sometimes gave us more food, but anybody could do this. Other guys wrote articles and also got more rations, but I was especially singled out.

When I finally obtained my file under the Freedom of Information Act, I was able to find out who testified against me. Even some of the guys who had promised to protect me when I volunteered to represent them in the prison camp had come out against me. Years later, some of these same guys visited me in Memphis. I think they wanted to find out what I thought of them. But I did not think anything. I love them. We all suffered the same hard times. When they returned home, the government put a lot of pressure on them to talk about the Progressives and the twenty-one. They had families and they needed to save their own lives. They did not want to go to jail, so somebody had to be blamed. I was not there, so I became the convenient scapegoat.

Interestingly, the two prisoners from Memphis I had been closest to in the prison camp, the Boys from the Big M, never said anything bad about me. They were not Progressives like I was, but we had been so tight in the camps that we protected each other. After the war, they told the investigators that they did not know anything about my activities. After all, if you have not done anything wrong yourself, it is not necessary to lie about the next man. But some obviously had done things themselves that did not look good. I never wanted to retaliate against any of these guys, because they had already suffered enough. Everybody had. Just having been in the war was bad enough, especially when you had no business being there in the first place.

With all this testimony lined up against me, the army would have loved to put me behind bars for the rest of my life, but it discovered it could not try me again because of double jeopardy. It had already court-martialed me once, and it could not do so again for the same crime. In addition, because I was no longer in the army, it no longer held jurisdiction over me.[5] What's more, the military could not turn my case over to a civilian court, because I had not been a civilian when I allegedly did all these things. Someone then decided that the House Un-American Activities Committee (HUAC) should investigate me as a traitor, after which a federal court could try me for treason.

····· ★ ·····

On July 28, 1966, just three weeks after I arrived back in the States, a U.S. marshal served a subpoena calling for me to appear before HUAC in Washington, D.C., to face several charges, including disrupting the morale of American fighting forces in Vietnam and inciting revolution in the United States. I was sent a ticket for my transportation to Washington and told to report on August 16, 1966, to Room 441 in the Cannon House Office Building.

I had no idea what to expect. I later learned that HUAC had subpoenaed several Vietnam War protesters, including Jerry Rubin and various other domestic radicals, to testify before the committee beginning on the same day I was to report. The committee planned to recommend a bill "to make it a criminal offense to interfere with troop movements, distribute propaganda affecting troop morale, or provide aid to hostile powers."

I knew I was in trouble. After all, the committee members would not have subpoenaed me if they were planning to do something nice for me. Nevertheless, I did nothing to prepare for the hearings, except to tell Lin that if I did not return, she should take the children and go to Utica, New York, and live with the Wills family, because Kai-yen Wills was her closest friend.

HUAC booked me into a hotel close to the Cannon Office Building. Each morning for a week, a government driver picked me up and drove me to the hearings and then took me back to the hotel when I was finished for the day.

When I walked into the Cannon Office Building that first day, the first thing I noticed were several fully armed policemen lined up outside of Room 441, which was a small room where apparently witnesses were initially questioned before the committee put them on display in the large public hearings room. I figured I did not have much of a chance and that I would probably be marched off to jail, but I was determined to tell the truth.

I began by telling the committee that I had come back to the States to work, take care of my family, and live a decent life. Then I said, "I'm glad to appear before your committee because this gives me an opportunity to defend myself. I do not feel I have done anything wrong. I want to be here, so you do not need those policemen to watch me. I'm not going anywhere." I did not see the policemen after that.

As I recall, there were four people waiting to question me in Room 441. I sat down across from them at this long conference table. They all had expressionless faces, and I had no idea what they were thinking. It was like talking to a wall. Even when I tried to be funny, they never changed their expressions. Nobody ever laughed except me. But after we got started, I relaxed. I figured if they had already made up their minds about my guilt, nothing I said would change their minds, so I just tried to make the best of a bad situation.

They began by asking if I wanted a lawyer. I told them, "No, I'll represent myself because I've not committed any crime. If I had committed a crime, I would need a lawyer, but since I have not, why should I get a lawyer?" I was the only one who knew what I had done all those years I lived outside of the United States, and no lawyer could have explained this to the committee members better than I. I also did not want a lawyer who might try to defend me by twisting things. What's more, I had no money, and whether I won or lost, I would have to pay the lawyer. Finally, if the government assigned me one of its own lawyers, he would have been working for them, and I would not have trusted him. So my strategy was simply to tell the unvarnished truth.

They asked me all kinds of questions about my past activities, but they were most interested in my anti–Vietnam War broadcasts. They asked if I had contacted any "domestic subversive groups" that opposed the war. I told them I had not, which was true. They then advised me not to mix with any subversive groups, and they named off a lot of them.

Actually, just days after we arrived in Memphis, several civil rights and antiwar groups had contacted me. When they asked me to join them, I told them, "I don't know what you're doing, and I don't care, but I'm not going to join your group. The government already suspects me of subversion, so that would give them even more ammunition. They would insist that Communists had infiltrated your organizations, which would further jeopardize your cause." I later realized that this had been a good decision, because these groups would have suspected the government had offered me a deal to gather information on them.

During their questioning, I looked committee members in the eye and simply repeated everything I had said in Hong Kong, on the boat, and in Honolulu. Whatever they asked, I answered them truthfully. They were really shocked and surprised. Evidently the truth was the last thing they expected from me. They thought I would deny everything or try to hide behind the Fifth Amendment. But I knew the best defense was just to tell them what I did and why, and then let them decide if I had committed treason.

They asked me why I hated America and what made me do what I did. I responded by going into great detail about how our white officers had sacrificed the all-black 503rd Field Artillery just before I was captured, costing the lives of so many good men. I told them:

> I will always be angry about this! When you get that many men killed for no reason at all, I can never forget or forgive. You do not have to be a general to know that during a retreat you first move out your heavy artillery. Then you move out your lighter weapons. Everyone also knows that an artillery unit needs infantry to protect it, but the infantry that was supposed to defend us was ordered out with the light artillery, leaving us practically defenseless to face the attacking Chinese. We did not stand a chance, and we got wiped out. I am sure we were sacrificed because we were black, which made us worthless and expendable in their eyes, and I have been angry about this ever since.

After I said this, nobody on the committee said anything for a long time. I then described how, when the Chinese attacked us, the white captain in charge of our battery, jumped into his jeep and just sat there:

> He didn't even fight. His jeep was at the head of the column, and a Molotov cocktail hit it. The driver jumped out and ran, but the white captain never moved. He just sat there and burned to death. I think he froze because he was scared stiff.

I also described how the Chinese forces that captured us first interrogated our officers and got all the information they needed from them:

> Our Chinese captors told us, "Your officers are weak and told us everything." So we enlisted men did not have to tell them anything because they already knew everything about our units, including when we arrived in Korea. So who betrayed us? Some of these officers who were trying to save their hides were West Point boys who had sworn to divulge nothing but name, rank, and serial number.

The committee then accused me of having collaborated while I was in the prison camp, but again I defended myself:

> I did not collaborate with the enemy. I cooperated with them, and that's very different than collaboration. If you were in that situation, what would you have done? Are you going to fight the man who has the gun? It was in the best interest of every prisoner to cooperate. We were prisoners. We had fought the war, but now we were captives, and it was a question of our own survival. I fought as hard as I could, but I lost, and when I became a prisoner, I had to consider my own life. I think all of you might well have done the same thing.

The committee's major charge against me was that I had disrupted the morale of the American fighting forces in Vietnam and incited revolution in the U.S. with my broadcasts to the American soldiers in Vietnam. I told the committee this was simply untrue:

> I did not talk to your army in Vietnam. I made it clear in my broadcast that I was addressing only the black soldiers in Vietnam, and I strongly believe I had every right to talk to them. I was not trying to hide anything, because I even gave my name, rank, and serial number. If I had been trying to keep my identity a secret, I would not have done that.

When one of the committee members asked me if I had been forced to make those broadcasts, I told him, "No way! I asked the Vietnamese if I could do so." Then he asked me if someone had written the text for me. This made me so angry that I told him, "You mean you don't think I am intelligent enough to write something like that myself?"

Another committeeman asked me, "Why did you choose to go to China, which is a Communist country and an enemy of America?" I told him:

> I had the right to go to any country that would honor my quest for freedom, equality, education, and happiness. Are you suggesting that whites have the right to go all over the world doing whatever it takes to obtain these things, but as a black man I do not have the same right? After all, I had already served my country, fighting to the bitter end, so I do not believe I owe it anything more.

We had committee sessions in the morning, after which I was free most afternoons. In the evening I usually ate dinner with some senator or other top government official, who was fishing for information about China and communism. They were like vultures, and they wanted to pick me clean. Somebody, probably from the FBI, would come to my hotel and say, "Senator or Representative So-and-So invites you to dinner." A congressman and usually some of his aides would then take me to dinner and ask me all kinds of questions about China. When one of them asked me about China's military and war production, I told him, "They've got a huge army, much larger than the Americans'. Even their militia is larger than our army, and they are well trained." I had observed army units training just outside of Beijing, and their training was superior to anything I had received in the military. So I told him, "You'd better think twice before you consider attacking China." I didn't say it, but I thought to myself, You had your hands full in Korea, so how are you going to defeat China? China would just swallow you up.

One senator asked, "What do the people think of communism? Do they support their government? Will they ever attempt to overthrow it?"

I told him, "The Chinese people support their government because the Communists have done a lot for them. They are living much better now than they were before the revolution, so they are not thinking about overthrowing their government anytime in the near future."

On my last day before the committee, I was beginning to get tired, and I said, "I'm not going to answer any more questions. You can do what you like with me. If you want to shoot me, do it, but I'm not going to answer any more questions. I'm through." They sent me out of the room for maybe ten minutes. Then they called me back and told me, "You're free to go. We've dismissed the charges."

I was surprised and I asked, "You mean I'm free to go home?"

They said, "We may have to call you back, but you are now free to return home."

I felt great, like I had won my case. The committee even gave me $100, I guess for the time I had to spend with them, and one of the investigators even took me to a go-go bar that night where the girls danced in cages.

The committee never interrogated me in the main hearings room, where the media and public would have heard my testimony, and it certainly could have ordered me to be tried for treason in a federal court; instead, it dropped all charges.

There were several possible reasons why the committee decided not to go after me publicly. As an open and creditable witness who used the truth to explain his actions, I think I might have disarmed the committee members, who were more accustomed to a different kind of witness. Then, too, if my case received national attention, my testimony would have impacted the black community. After all, when I made those broadcasts, I was trying to save the lives of black soldiers, and at the time of my testimony we still had black men being killed in Vietnam. In addition, in 1966 the civil rights movement was very much on the minds of all African Americans, and they would have to think about my words. Clearly, if all blacks had been free and enjoying the same rights that whites took for granted, the government could have prosecuted me in front of them, but this was certainly not the case.

Finally, with the growing antiwar sentiment, social unrest, and urban riots spreading across the country, the government did not want the kind of publicity my trial might have given black leaders and radicals, let alone the impact it might have had on black soldiers in the field.[6]

After the hearings, a committee investigator told me that they were going to set up a school to teach about communism and they wanted me to serve as an adviser and possibly an instructor. He asked me to write an essay on what I thought of communism, which I did. This was, of course, before Richard Nixon went to China, so I said it was foolish for the United States not to establish diplomatic relations with China:

> You are turning down a great opportunity. The British, the French, and everybody else is establishing some kind of relationship, but you are holding out. They are the ones who are going to do business with China, and you will be left out. Do you really think Chiang Kai-shek can represent the mainland Chinese?

· · · · · ★ · · · · ·

Even though HUAC had not sought a federal indictment for treason, there were still plenty of people who considered me a traitor, and this made life very difficult for us back in Memphis. For example, the day after I got back from Washington, I was ordered to report to the local FBI office in the downtown federal building. A man whose first name was Lawrence headed the local FBI, and I had several meetings with him. He wanted to make sure I understood the FBI was keeping me under surveillance, and it did for at least ten years. I knew it tapped our telephone, because for years, whenever we picked up the receiver, there was always a brief delay before the dial tone.

My return to the States during the growing antiwar movement made me again reflect on what we had gone through in Korea. World War II had been so different because we were all united against the common enemy of fascism. But America had no real need to be in Korea and Vietnam, because neither was a threat to the United States. Germany had been a threat to the entire world. North Korea and North Vietnam were not planning to invade America, but Germany might well have. The Koreans and the Vietnamese should have been allowed to settle their own problems rather than us forcing our way of life on them. The people of every nation should have the right to decide for themselves how they want to live.

We certainly would never accept an outside country coming in and meddling in our internal affairs and telling us what kind of life we should live. We would not be America if we had not fought a revolution to free ourselves from British rule. If it was right for us to free ourselves from England, other nations should also have the right to free themselves from foreign oppressors, whoever they might be.

CHAPTER ELEVEN

Bootstrapping to the American Dream

Everybody was relieved when I got back to Memphis from Washington. I think my uncles were the happiest—except, of course, Lin. Unfortunately, after a few days, reality set in. We had nothing to live on but our meager savings. I thought I was entitled to my back pay, plus my soldier's deposits, which were in a savings account in a military bank. I asked the American Civil Liberties Union for help, and it spent two years representing me, but the government insisted the statute of limitations had run out on paying me any money. Well, the statute of limitations might have run out on my pay, but what about my money in the bank? How could there be a statute of limitation on savings? Even if I had received the money in my savings account, with some fifteen years of compounded interest, it would have been several thousand dollars. I finally asked for just this money, but the government refused to give me anything.

Using the Freedom of Information Act, the ACLU did obtain some of the government's documents on me, including those that pertained to the court-martial trial. The ACLU argued that the army's court-martial trial was illegal, and so I was entitled to an honorable discharge. But the government just gave them the runaround, shifting them from one branch to another. Finally, the government said all the records had been destroyed in a fire in St. Louis, and they no longer had any records on me. When the government refused to admit I even existed, I asked, "If I don't exist, why did you order me go to Washington, and why are you taxing me?"

Americans are generally forgiving people. No one will let me starve here in the United States where there's such prosperity.
—Clarence Adams, July 9, 1966

I can remember passing the door of the First Memphis National Bank. By this time I was so desperate that I even thought of robbing it. I was determined that I was not going to sit there and watch my family starve.
—Clarence Adams, six months later

After I got back from Washington, relations became increasingly strained at my mother's house. I had sent her approximately $2,000 out of my soldier's pay and my gambling winnings that she used to buy her house. I also gave her $1,000 out of our savings when we arrived in Memphis, so I thought we could stay with her for as long as we needed to. Our main support during these troubled times came from my uncle King Adams and his wife, Bea. I had always been very close to King, and Bea was very fond of Lin. Bea would often invite us over for a meal and then have a long conversation with Lin. Lin taught her how to cook Chinese, and she taught Lin how to cook American. At one of these dinners, Bea pressured Lin to talk about our financial situation and how things were at Toosie's house. Because she was so proud, Lin did not want to talk about money, but Bea, in addition to being very kind, was also persistent. She invited our family to stay with her for a week, just to give us a break from all the tension and unhappiness at Toosie's. That week turned into two weeks because Bea did not want us to leave. When we returned to Toosie's house, things only got worse. Toosie was angry that we enjoyed our stay at Bea's and told Lin that if we went there again, not to come back. So we went back to King and Bea's and lived with them for several months, until a distant relative named Estella Lee offered us her house because she was living in Detroit and needed someone to look after it. Initially, she said we did not have to pay rent, only the utilities. We thought she was being very generous. After a couple of months, however, she changed her mind and asked for rent, but I simply did not have the money to pay her.

These were terrible times for us. Our savings were running out, and although Bea quietly slipped Lin some money, we could not live off her and King's generosity. I had to find some kind of work to support my family. I wrote letters to several universities seeking employment in their departments of Asian studies teaching Mandarin Chinese, which was the official language of the People's Republic of China. When I first came back, I had received teaching feelers from UCLA and the University of Hawaii, but at the time I just wanted to go home and be left alone, so I ignored them. I even had letters of recommendation from influential friends in Hong Kong; but now it was too late, and no one wanted me. Some universities suggested I try schools closer to home, but hometown Memphis State turned me down flat.

I got my first job in September 1966 with a black insurance company called Union Protective. Toosie knew someone through church who helped me get in the door. At first, the company worried whether it was legal to hire someone like me. To them, a "turncoat" was some kind of traitor or criminal. They asked me to write to the government for permission to work, which I thought was absurd. Nevertheless, I wrote HUAC, and one of its investigators, Philip Manuel, answered, "It is my sincere hope that you are accepted by that firm if that is your desire, but please be advised that this committee is not authorized to grant or revoke clearances as such."

Union Protective knew it had me over a barrel, so it exploited me by giving me the housing projects, which was its worst assignment. My job was to collect overdue premiums from people who had no money. At first, I was bringing home almost $90 a week, but that amount became less and less. The company tried to force me to make up the difference when the people could no longer afford to pay their premiums. To make matters worse, I had bought a used Ford Valiant to make my insurance collections. This had really upset Lin because we had to take $800 out of what little was left of our meager savings. I knew nothing about the used car market, so I probably got ripped off. Now, I also had gas and insurance expenses for the car at a time when my income was going down and down.

I quit the insurance company after a little over a year because it was costing me more than I was making. My mother became so angry when I quit the job she had helped me get that she called us a bunch of ingrates and vowed she would never help us again even if we starved.

I looked for work for several weeks, but no one would hire me once they knew who I was. I finally was offered a job as a janitor, but again, someone recognized my name, and I was told I was overqualified. I was also informed that they needed someone who was willing to stay for a long time. I assured them that I would stay for at least a year. I also told them I had a wife and two children to feed. I actually begged them for the job, but nothing worked. I even asked our family minister, Reverend S. A. Owen, if I could work at the church in exchange for food and rent money, but he also turned me down.

After so many failures, I became deeply depressed. For days I refused to go out. But Lin pushed me to keep trying. I still remember the day the two of us went to an employment agency. After I filled out the first half of the necessary papers, I came to the question, "Have you ever been dishonorably discharged from the army?" I threw the pen and papers on the table and said to Lin, "Let's go home. It's no use."

In February of 1968 I went back to Union Protective and begged to be re-hired. They assigned me to a territory in Knoxville, Tennessee, which was four hundred miles from Memphis. Unfortunately, Knoxville was no better than Memphis. I still could not make enough to support the family, and things went from bad to worse. One day my mother went to Lin and offered her two dollars for food for the children but told her not to spend any of it on me. Lin was so distraught that she called me in tears. She told me all our money was gone and that she and the children had nothing to eat. In the middle of the night in a raging snowstorm, I drove back to Memphis.

After I got back, a kind neighbor asked her church to donate a food basket for us, and that temporarily saved us. My daughter Della remembers those dark days and understood what was happening. Lin would fix a peanut butter sandwich and cut it in half. One half was for Della to take to school, and the other half I took with me when I left the house to look for work. Lin often did not eat lunch.

My stepfather, Fred, was one of the few who really wanted to help us after we came home, but there was nothing he could do. He was not the boss in his own house, and my mother would have made things bad for him if he tried to help. Fred was by then retired, sick with diabetes, and living on social security. I told him, "I appreciate your generosity and willingness to help us, but forget it. There's no point in you getting thrown out of the house on my behalf." He was a good man, and I owed him a lot. When I was younger, I did not see it that way, but as I got older, I began to understand that he had done everything he could for me, and for that I still respect him.

This went on week after week, month after month. I can remember passing the door of the First Memphis National Bank. By this time I was so desperate that I even thought of robbing it. I was determined that I was not going to sit there and watch my family starve. But just when things looked completely hopeless, our luck finally changed.

During one of my futile searches for work, I was exhausted from walking the streets, and I entered a small coffee shop called Harlem House. I smiled at the waitress and said, "I have no money. I'm just going to sit here and rest a little if that's all right with you." She looked at me and said, "Don't worry. Have a cup of coffee on us." I was gratefully sipping my coffee when I overheard a conversation at the other end of the counter: "Did you hear that Johnnie Walker Red just died?"

His companion asked, "Which Johnnie?"

"Oh, you know, the fellow who drove the delivery truck for the House of Typography. He died yesterday of ptomaine poisoning."

I thought to myself, It's Monday. If Johnnie died yesterday, his job must still be available. I immediately took off for a telephone booth and looked up the address for the House of Typography, which was a printing company. There it was, 359 North Second Street, only a few blocks from where I was standing.

I got over there as fast as my feet would carry me, and I was hired on the spot. After I punched in, someone took me out back and said, "Here's your truck." I looked inside the cab and saw that it was a standard shift, which I had never learned to drive. All I could think of was that army fire truck I had backed into the wall in Korea. I felt my palms go all sweaty. I asked one of the guys how the gears worked, and he drew a diagram with a brief explanation. That was it. I was ready for my first delivery. I slowly pulled out of the lot in first gear. I looked back and saw the boss standing on the dock watching me. I did not dare try to shift gears, until I got around the corner. Then I stalled right in the middle of a busy intersection. I was trying to get the truck restarted, when a policeman came running up and yelled, "Boy, what's wrong with you? Move that truck!" I started to panic, but then I said, "Sir, there's some problems with this truck, and my boss asked me to drive it to the repair shop." That, of course, was a lie, but it worked, and he waved me on. I drove off in fits and starts, but by the end of the day I had become a real truck driver.

I never asked what my pay was going to be because I did not really care as long as I had a job. I worked hard and never complained about anything. When I was between deliveries, I did not chat with the other black drivers; in fact, I did not mingle with any of my co-workers because I feared they might find out who I was and tell the boss. Instead, I found a mop and began to clean the back room and the filthy bathroom. I continued doing this for several weeks; then one morning Bob Dawson, who owned the shop along with his brother Gary, came up to me and said, "We're delighted you cleaned those toilets. They haven't been cleaned in a year." I also repainted the entire back office, and I made sure I was always at work on time. If the boss called me at home for overtime, I never turned him down, although some of the other guys would, especially if it was a Sunday.

The other drivers made it clear that I was making it difficult for them because doing all this extra work made them look bad. I didn't care, because I had only one thought in mind: I'm not losing this job! I've got to feed my family, and I want the boss to know that I'm willing to work harder than anybody else.

I started at $1.50 an hour, but after the boss complimented me on my hard work, he gave me a ten-cent raise, which brought me up to the minimum wage of $1.60. But just as I was congratulating myself on my good luck, my boss surprised me by asking, "How does your wife like it here in America?"

"She likes it all right, sir," I mumbled, and quickly walked away.

"Oh my God!" I thought. "I've just lost another job."

For days I tried to avoid any contact with Bob, wondering when he was going to fire me. But nothing ever happened. Soon I got another raise. Although it was only ten cents more an hour, it meant a lot more than that to me.

I eventually became good friends with Bob. His two young daughters were crazy about me, and often came to the shop and asked me to tell them stories about China and other far-off lands. Sometimes I had to tell him, "Mr. Bob, you have to get your daughters out of here so I can get some work done." After several promotions, Bob told me he was going to make me a monotype caster, which was one of the highest-paid positions in the factory. He also told the typesetters and proofreaders, who were white, that they would have to teach me. They did not want to because by now they knew I was the Clarence Adams who had gone to China. They also thought I was too dumb to learn, because casting monotype was highly skilled work that normally called for a five-year apprenticeship. Three months later I was casting type, and this made them furious.

The white workers now had to use typefaces I made on the linotype machine, but they refused on the grounds that I was not a member of the union. At that time the Printers' Union of Memphis was lily white, and several times it turned down my application for membership. Nevertheless, Bob stuck to his guns and insisted I be allowed to work on the linotype machine. Some union members were also upset about not being paid extra for some training they were forced to do. In addition, they wanted a big increase in their regular pay. When Bob and Gary refused, they went out on strike, and this strike, which began in 1971, lasted thirteen months.

I did not want to be one of the causes of the strike, so the day it began I said to Bob, "It's up to you, Mr. Bob. This is your shop, and if you do not want me to work here, I'll leave. But if you say I can come in and work, nobody can stop me."

He looked at me and said, "You are always welcome to work in my shop. I'll see you tomorrow morning."

The next morning the striking workers brought in at least twenty outside union members to support them. Most were big, strong, and mean, and of course all of them were white. The other blacks who worked for the House of Typography gathered on a street corner a couple of blocks away and watched because they were too terrified to come in to work.

When Bob arrived, these outsiders blocked the front door and started pushing and kicking him. Some called him a "nigger lover." When Bob resisted, several of them jumped him. His brother Gary came out of the factory and absorbed a few blows himself before he was able to drag Bob inside.

I was sitting in my car across the street watching all this. When the strikers spotted me, they waved their fists at me. I noticed that one of them had a baseball bat. I had a .22-caliber pistol in my pocket and a large butcher knife which I had hidden in a newspaper. I said to myself, "This is the moment of truth. It's too late to run away now." I thought about my family, and I really did want to get out of there, but I also knew I could not be a coward. I had never run from anything in my life, so I took a deep breath, pulled the knife out of the newspaper and the pistol out of my pocket, and slowly walked toward the picket line. I was so frightened that my whole body was shaking. As I moved closer, I shouted, "Tennessee has a right-to-work law, and you can't stop me from making a living. I have a family to feed, just like you!"

Holding the pistol in one hand and the knife in the other, I moved steadily toward them. I looked directly at the first guy blocking my path and in a trembling voice said, "I can't whip all of you, but if you so much as touch me, I'll keep shooting as long as I've got bullets, and I'll keep stabbing as long as I can hold this knife."

The picket line suddenly collapsed. The men stepped back one after the other, like the Red Sea parting for Moses. A kind of paralysis set in. Clearly, none of them was prepared for a black man to stand up to them, and I could see in their faces they were afraid of getting hurt. Only after I got into the factory did they suddenly flock to the back windows, where they spent the rest of the day shouting, "Commie! Nigger! Red! Go back to China!"

All day long I had to listen to them screaming, but they did not dare come in. When I left for lunch, I went out the back door. A striker I knew started walking toward me. The gun was in my pocket, but I had the butcher knife in my hand. When he got right in front of me, I said, "Hey, John, you better get out of the way because I'm not walking around you. I'll go through you but not around you." When he was within an arm's length of me, he said, "Hey, there's no need for bloodshed," and he turned away. At that moment I was thinking, I hope he moves, because if he doesn't, I'm going to have to kill him. I would have done it, too. I was pushed against the wall with no escape and was ready to die right then and there. Incidentally, John, who lived across the river in Arkansas's Crittenden County, was one of only two whites Bob hired back after the strike. We later got to know each other and chatted like nothing had ever happened.

The strikers wanted to do away with me in the worst way, and they were almost successful. Strangely enough, what saved my life was an exhibition the Chinese Ping-Pong team played in Memphis. An American team had gone to China in the spring of 1971 as part of President Nixon's Ping-Pong diplomacy.

Now the Chinese team was making a reciprocal ten-city tour of the U.S., which included coming to Memphis in the spring of 1972. Lin called me at work and told me that Representative Alvin King, who was a state representative from Memphis and a friend of the family, had invited us to attend. Lin was thrilled because she had not seen anyone from mainland China for six long years, and she was terribly homesick. I had committed to working overtime that night, so I told Lin to go alone. After all, I had never turned down Bob when he asked me to work, and I did not want to start now. But Lin was very insistent and told me in no uncertain terms, "I have gone through a lot of things by myself, but this time I want you to be with me." So I asked Bob, and he said, "Of course. Go with your wife and have fun. I'll have J. C. help me." J. C. was a childhood friend of mine, and I had urged Bob to hire him to help out during the strike.

Lin and I went to the exhibition and afterwards went on a cruise on the Mississippi with the Chinese delegation. We drank champagne and listened to B. B. King play the blues. I enjoyed talking to the Chinese delegation, and especially its leader, Swong Se Doon. We spoke to each other in Chinese, while an FBI agent, who obviously had been assigned to keep an eye on me, stood behind us recording our conversation. I could see the tape recorder hanging from his chest, so we only talked in general terms about my time in China and the city of Memphis. Neither of us wanted to say anything political, and everything went smoothly. When we said good-bye, Swong Se Doon told me he was delighted to meet me because I was the only Chinese-speaking American he had met who was not officially sanctioned by the government.

While Lin and I were enjoying ourselves with the Chinese delegation, J. C. made his delivery to the Greyhound bus station. When he came out to the truck, two white guys jumped him, put a gun to his head, and told him to start driving. Of course, they thought they had me, and there's no doubt what they were planning to do. They drove J. C. to a deserted spot under a Mississippi River bridge, pointed the gun at him, and said, "We're going to kill you, Clarence Adams!" J. C. swore to them they had the wrong person and begged them to spare his life. When he finally was allowed to show them his driver's license, they drove off in his truck and left him under the bridge. The company had no idea what had happened to him and notified the police. When the police finally located him, he was just walking back and forth under the bridge in a state of shock. I did not find out what happened until the next day when I arrived at work. Bob told me that J. C. was shaking so hard when the police found him that he could barely tell them what happened.

J. C. quit the company because he said working there was too dangerous.

If I had made the delivery, I would have been dead. The police, of course, did nothing, but they knew it had to be someone who supported the strikers, and certainly the strikers knew who did it. At that time there was nowhere a black could turn if someone committed a crime against him. The police were never going to help blacks, and neither were the courts. You could not report to a white law enforcement officer that a white man had committed a crime against you. Hell, the white policeman would make it rough on you for even suggesting a white man had attacked you.

I ended up working at the House of Typography for six years, but even after I quit to open up our first restaurant, I had the keys to the shop for at least two more years. Every time I tried to give Bob or Gary the keys, they told me to keep them. Even when Lin and I were busy with our first Chop Suey House, if they needed me to work, I would go down and help out. I would tell them, "You don't have to pay me. I'll work for nothing." But they insisted, and they paid me more after I officially quit than when I was working there. Maybe on a Sunday they would have a rush job from Chicago or St. Louis that needed to be finished and sent out on Monday morning. I would run the stuff on the machine, the bosses would set it, and we'd have it in the mail first thing Monday morning. They'd send me a check, but I'd send it back. Finally, Bob said, "You've got to cash these checks or you'll mess up my books." I just wanted them to know how much I appreciated them giving me that job when I needed one so badly. I owed them everything. We are still friends; in fact, when Bob's daughters got ready to marry, each of them brought her fiancé over to meet me.

Above all else, Lin and I wanted to have our own place. In the spring of 1967 we were able to move into an attic apartment on Foster Street. We had two rooms and a very small kitchen, but the rent was very cheap, and that's why we took it. It was in a poor, although not necessarily dangerous, area. However, because Della and Louis looked different, the neighborhood kids were constantly teasing and threatening them. Della was older, so I taught her how to box and become a street fighter so she could survive. She became very good at taking care of herself; in fact, she still is. All this represented a major transformation from the protected, princess-like existence she had enjoyed in China. Now she was being forced to live and survive in the "hood." This was difficult for me to observe, and I constantly promised Della that one day she would have all kinds of wonderful things. She loved hearing this, and although I never got rich, I did well enough so that by the time she got to high school, she had lots of nice clothes and a brand new car. I was also able to pay for her college education.

We stayed in that little apartment on Foster Street for several months. We continued to save, and soon were able to buy our first house for $9,500. It was on Mallory Street in an area called Longview, which was a fairly decent neighborhood. We had a thousand dollars in the bank, and the down payment and closing costs came to $1,000. We drew out $999, leaving one dollar to keep the account open. We now owned a home of our own, but we still needed to improve our financial situation.

I started working a second job in 1968. I would work eight hours a day at the House of Typography and another four hours late at night unloading trucks for Sergeant's Truck Line. By this time, Lin's English had improved enough so she was also able to get a job sewing suitcases for the Trojan Luggage Company. The owners of the company appreciated what a good worker she was, until the day I picked her up from work. When they saw that she was married to a black man, they immediately let her go. In 1969 Lin got a job with the federal Head Start program, and the next year she became a teacher's aide and a part-time physical education instructor in the Memphis Public Schools. She was much better educated than any of the teachers she worked with, and they resented that sometimes she corrected their work, especially in math. In 1972 we opened our first Chop Suey House on Airways Boulevard, and she quit her school job.

We stayed in the Mallory house until 1974, when we sold it for $16,000 and put the money down on a $29,000 house on Windward Street in White Haven. We sold this house for $50,000 in 1986 and purchased our current house for $130,000, which is in the suburban Wyndike neighborhood in southeast Shelby County. It is a very quiet and safe neighborhood of mostly middle-class whites. When we moved in, the police used to follow me home every night, because no black could walk through that area without the Neighborhood Watch people calling the police. The police followed me for a long time before they realized I was a homeowner. The neighbors on both sides were white, and one was chief of police in Bartlett, Tennessee, which is just north of Memphis. So everyone was keeping an eye on us.

I loved it when these white joggers would run past our house just to see the black family that had moved into the neighborhood. I'd look at them, and they'd look the other way. Finally, they got used to me because I started jogging too. That was something I had never done before. I became just like white people. I started jogging by their houses and starring at them. Now they know me, and we have no problems. Like all Americans, when blacks make more money, they move up. We now have at least six black families in our neighborhood. All of them are middle class, and most own their own businesses.

All those years while we were trying to better ourselves, we lived a very frugal existence. Lin and I did not buy anything for ourselves, just a few things for the kids. The only thing I purchased was work clothes and shoes, and I bought my clothes at the Goodwill Store, where you could get work pants for maybe a dollar and shirts for fifty cents. We saved every penny we could. Lin handled the money and kept the books. She was much better at this than I. I'm a spendthrift, but if you put money in her hands, she'll squeeze the eagle off of it; in fact, that eagle would began to scream. She made all the decisions on what to do with our savings. I would just make the money, take my check home, put it in her hands, and never see it again. Even today I do not know what we have. She has done a wonderful job. We are a good team, and it took both of us to get where we are.

Lin and I eventually owned eight restaurants, including four of them at the same time, but it was a struggle when we first went into the restaurant business. Early on we got so far behind with our bills that we desperately needed $2,000 to save the business. Uncle Archie Adams had never married and possessed a healthy bank account and a very good retirement from the Ford Motor Company in Detroit. He was my youngest uncle and the only one who could spare the money. He was not much older than I, and we had spent a lot of time together after he came out of the army. I called Archie and asked for a loan, but I also had to tell him I did not know when I could pay it back. He immediately sent the money and told me, "Whenever you can, repay me." When things began to go better, I paid him back, with the same interest he would have received if he had left his money in the bank.

We put a recreation center in the back of our first Chop Suey House containing all kinds of games the neighborhood kids would pay to play, but I closed it down when the older kids began coming in and taking money from the younger ones. Matters came to a head when I got in a fight with one of the older kids. He was maybe eighteen and considerably bigger than I. He was taking money from the younger kids, and I ordered him to leave. He refused, and he put up his fists and told me, "You can't make me leave." That was a mistake. I grabbed him, threw him up against the wall, and hit him. He fell down, and when he got up he said he was going to go get his daddy. I told him, "Please, don't do that. I'm going to let you go, but if your daddy comes back with you, I'm going to kill him. If you want your daddy to live, don't bring him here." About fifteen minutes later he came back with his daddy. In the meantime I had gone up front and grabbed my .357 Magnum. When his

In July 1972 Clarence and Lin Adams opened their first Chop Suey House.
They would open seven more restaurants.

daddy walked in, I told him, "Look, your boy is wrong. He was taking money from these younger kids, and when I asked him to leave, he refused to go. All he had to do was leave and nothing would have happened. I have a business here, and you have to respect this. I opened up this arcade so the kids in the neighborhood could have a place to feel free to play without danger, and I will not allow any older boy to take advantage of them. I hope you can understand this and explain it to your son, because I really don't want to hurt you."

I had a gun, and he had nothing. He finally realized he had to go, but not before he cursed me out. He called me everything he could think of. I told him, "That's all right. As long as you leave, you can call me anything you want, but don't come back." He was still cursing me as he went out the door and down the alley. I did not want any more of that, so I had the machines removed. I hated to lose the revenue, because I made enough off those games to pay the rent and utilities and have some money left over.

We have now been in business for twenty-two years, and we have outlasted a lot of people. We are now down to a single restaurant, the Chop Suey House we opened on Airways Avenue back in 1972. During all those years, we saw a lot of businesses, white and black, that did not last. But even when the economy went bad, we managed to hold on. The economy is still bad in Memphis, with businesses closing every day, but we continue making enough money to survive.

· · · · · ★ · · · · ·

I am now closing in on my seventieth birthday, and I have occasionally wondered how different my life would have been if I had returned to Memphis in 1953 instead of going to China. I would have been a twenty-four-year-old African-American high school dropout, with few opportunities to create a successful life. The civil rights movement was just beginning and would not have a significant impact on Memphis for many years. I might have made it as a boxer, but only the few who reach the top make any kind of living. More likely, I would have gone back to hustling tips as a hotel porter or room service boy, and I seriously doubt I would have been able to complete seven years of college or be offered a job similar to the one I had at the Foreign Languages Press in Beijing. I also would never have met those African diplomats who made such a profound impression on me, and I certainly would not have met anyone like Lin.

Many social and racial changes have occurred in the United States since my return in 1966. However, some of these changes are not as pronounced as they appear to most white people. Memphis is a good example. The overt racism of the past is no longer acceptable. I can now walk in any park, shop at any store, and sit wherever I please in any movie theater or restaurant. I can even eat at Justine's, if I have enough money. But such surface changes do not mean that racism has disappeared; it is just more subtle. I recently called a food supplier for an order. He could tell from my voice that I was black, and he asked for a higher price for the items I wanted than he did when Lin called him a short time later. When something like this happens, the old resentment and anger wells up inside me, just as it has throughout my life.

Covert racism means it exists, but nobody is responsible, and it can be even more frustrating than the old-fashioned Ku Klux Klan kind. At least in the old days, you knew where you stood with whites. Today you have no idea what their true feelings are or what they are planning for you. Della recently asked me, "Do you now hate all white people? After all, you have many white friends to whom you are very close, and your best friend in China, Morris Wills, is white."

I told her, "Della, it's not a racial thing so much as it is cultural. White is not simply a skin color; it's an idea, a way of acting, and because of this I will never completely trust whites to the day I die."

It was true I was very close to several whites during my lifetime. There was Peach, who had tried to help me during that horrible death march to the permanent prison camp when I could barely walk. I also had white friends in the camp itself, and in China I was very close to Morris Wills and Richard Corden. Then there was Bob Dawson and his brother, who gave me a job when I so desperately needed one. These were individuals I liked, and even admired, but they saw me as Clarence Adams, an individual, rather than as some universal black man who was to be shunned or controlled.

I greatly admire Malcolm X, and I read his autobiography several times. I found it very telling that it was only after he went to the Middle East and met white Moslems that he changed his mind about the "White Devils," as he called them. At home, he continued to hate and distrust white Americans, and I have to agree with him. I also agreed with Malcolm in his dislike of Martin Luther King's message of nonviolence and passive integration. I would never degrade King personally or say he was ineffective, but it was not until Malcolm X, the Black Panthers, and the urban riots really frightened whites that they became more willing to accept King as a black leader.

I used to argue with other blacks about racial issues. Too many of them were not ready to stand up for their rights. I'd call them Uncle Toms, because they were afraid to say anything. They were all for the civil rights movement, but only as long as somebody else did the fighting and bleeding. Some of these same blacks also resented that I owned my own business. They thought I held myself above them and was putting on airs because I had lived in China and had a college education. Others took issue with the kind of work I did. So-called white-collar workers would come into the Chop Suey House and ask me, "How can you do this kind of manual labor?"

I would answer, "Dammit, I'm my own boss. Can any of you say that?"

Maybe that is what my life was all about. I always wanted to be my own boss, and not just at work. This is undoubtedly why I was always so quick to react in anger whenever anyone tried to tell me what to do. I was determined to be my own person and control my own destiny, and no one else was going to define who I was or tell me what I was supposed to do. When you think about it, isn't this what America is supposed to be all about?

Shortly before he died, I had a very revealing conversation with my father. We had often talked after work at one of our restaurants over our customary glass of Old Grand Dad, but this conversation was different. Seven years earlier he had been diagnosed with emphysema, which was now in its final stages. He knew the end was near, and he wanted to assess his life in a more positive way, without the disappointment and bitterness he so often expressed.

During many of our previous conversations, he often denigrated his many accomplishments. In spite of being an educated man and owning eight restaurants and a nice home with plenty of creature comforts, he would still insist, "I am a failure."

I'd tell him, "You're crazy. You're not a failure. You started from nothing, and look at the life you've had."

But he would insist, "Look, I did not get what I wanted."

I never could pinpoint what it was that he wanted, other than, "I failed your mother. I brought her here, and she had to work harder in America than she ever did in China. That was not what I wanted for her." He would have tears in his eyes when he spoke of how he had failed my mother.

Religion may also have played a role in this final talk. My father always claimed he was an atheist, even though he was brought up a Baptist. What he really wanted, of course, was to control his own life. He'd often say to me, "God and I have an understanding. I'm not going to try and fool Him, because He knows I'm a rotten son of a bitch, but I'm not the most rotten son of a bitch in the world." When I would say, "You were really blessed" or "God was really looking out for you," he'd say, "Don't worry about it. The two of us have our understanding." He now told me that God had informed him that he had little time left.

Intellectually he understood that he had transformed that little black kid hustling pennies on the streets of Memphis into someone who had a college degree from a foreign university, spoke fluent Chinese, associated with fascinating people from around the world, read widely, translated many books, and was a proud and successful businessman. He understood all this in his mind, but deep inside he really did not see that person as himself. Somehow, in his darker moments, he was still the same Skippy who could never please

Lin and Clarence Adams shortly before his death in 1999.

his mother or the world around him. Conversely, he was also afraid of being too successful or, better said, afraid of becoming something he was not.

But in this final conversation he said, "Della, you know what? I think we did okay. Looking back at our lives, we did do a lot of things right. Some good things happened, and I'm happy with this." After that, he and my mom did not argue so much. They also started doing more things together. A couple of months before he died, he told her, "You know, Lin, I think we've had a pretty good and interesting life together." About that, I had no argument with him.

Clarence and Lin Adams celebrating daughter Della's wedding on August 16, 1998, just thirteen months before Clarence died.

CLARENCE CECIL ADAMS TIME LINE

January 4, 1929
   Clarence Cecil Adams is born in Memphis, Tennessee
September 11, 1947
   Joins the U.S. Army
December 1947–December 1948
   First tour of duty in Korea
December 1948–June 1950
   Tour of duty in Japan
June 25, 1950
   North Korea invades South Korea; Adams's enlistment is extended for one
   year
August 1950
   Lands in South Korea
November 30, 1950
   Captured by Chinese troops
December 10, 1950
   Arrives at Camp 5 on the Yalu River on the northern border of North Korea
July 27, 1953
   Signing of Korean War Armistice
August 23, 1953
   Chooses not to join the liberated American prisoners
September 3, 1953
   Last American prisoners are repatriated
January 23, 1954
   Final deadline set by the Neutral Nations Repatriation Commission for
   those choosing not to go home to change their minds
February 24, 1954
   First crosses the border into China
February–March, 1954
   In Taiyüan, China, for indoctrination and initial education
1954–1956
   Attends People's University, Beijing
1956–1961
   Attends Wuhan University in Wuhan

December 20, 1957
Marries Liu Lin Feng
January 3, 1959
Birth of daughter Della
May 1961
Graduates from Wuhan University with majors in Chinese language and political economy; moves to Beijing
1961–1966
Works for the Foreign Languages Press in Beijing
August 4, 1964
Birth of son Louis
August 15, 1965
Radio Hanoi broadcasts Adams's antiwar message to African American soldiers in Vietnam
May 26, 1966
Crosses the border into Hong Kong after having decided to return to the United States
June 29, 1966
Arrives in Honolulu; holds a press conference the next day
July 4, 1966
Lands in San Francisco
July 8, 1966
Secretly arrives home in Memphis
July 28, 1966
U.S. marshal serves Adams a subpoena to appear before the House Un-American Activities Committee on August 16
August 16–20, 1966
Testifies before the House Un-American Activities Committee in closed hearings
September 1966–Christmas 1967
Works for Union Protective Insurance
February 1968
Works again for Union Protective Insurance
June 1968
Begins working for House of Typography
August 1968
Purchases first home in Memphis, on Mallory Street
July 1972
Opens first Chop Suey House Restaurant in Memphis

November 1973
    Purchases second home in Memphis, on Windward
1974
    Opens Mei Lin Chinese Restaurant
1976
    Opens second Chop Suey House
1983
    Opens third Chop Suey House
1984
    Opens fourth Chop Suey House
1984
    Opens Rhapsody International Cuisine Restaurant
May 1986
    Purchases third home in Memphis, on Green Belt
1989
    Opens China House Restaurant
1990
    Opens Beijing Chinese Restaurant
September 17, 1999
    Clarence Cecil Adams dies at age 70 from complications of acute
    emphysema

NOTES

1. SKIPPY

1. David M. Tucker, *Memphis Since Crump: Bossism, Blacks, and Civic Reformers, 1948–1968* (Knoxville: University of Tennessee Press, 1980), 14.

2. Ibid.

3. Virginia Pasley, *21 Stayed: The Story of the American GI's Who Chose Communist China-Who They Were and Why They Stayed* (New York: Farrar, Straus and Cudahy, 1955), 132–34. Pasley ignored the reasons why the three African American POWs decided to go to China, and her description of the other eighteen was equally distorted; for example, she wrote, "So far as possible the Communists chose the twenty-one from what they termed the peasant and the beggar class: poor marginal farm dwellers and town-bred relief clients" (229). In truth, the economic, social, and educational background of the twenty-one was as varied as that of their fellow soldiers.

4. Lucie E. Campbell was indeed famous in the development of gospel music, having composed more than one hundred gospel songs, including "The Lord Is My Shepherd," "Heavenly Sunshine," "The King's Highway," "Touch Me Lord Jesus," and "He Understands, He'll Say, 'Well Done.'" So well connected was she in gospel circles that she was able to help the careers of promising young singers and composers such as Marian Anderson and J. Robert Bradley. Both she and brother Charles were graduates of Booker T. Washington High School, although at that time it was called Kortrecht High School. Only fourteen years old when she graduated valedictorian, she immediately begin teaching at Carnes Avenue Grammar School. In 1911 she returned to Kortrecht High School as an American history and English teacher. She also earned her B.A. from Rust College in Holy Springs, Mississippi, and her M.A. from Tennessee Agricultural and Industrial State College. She was named the music director of the National Sunday and Baptist Training Union Congress in Memphis in 1915 and remained a driving force in the National Baptist Convention. She later served as vice president of the American Teachers Association and as president of the Tennessee Teachers Association. In addition, she was a civil rights activist who crusaded for the elimination of salary and benefit inequities for black teachers. In 1960, just three years before her death, she married the Reverend C. R. Williams.

5. After Joe Louis knocked out Max Schmeling, white newspapers were either condescending or filled with warnings about what black celebrants might do. For example, a June 23, 1938, headline in the *New York Times* intoned, "Detroit Negroes Joyful: Sing and Dance in Streets to Celebrate Louis' Victory," while another stated, "Harlem

Celebrants Toss Varied Missiles." The *St. Louis Post Dispatch*'s headline for the same day blared, "Negroes Parade Here After Louis Victory: Cheers, Horns, Tub-Thumping Fill Air."

2. U.S. ARMY COMBAT SOLDIER

1. Adams was certainly familiar with the historical myths that African Americans were too cowardly or inept to bear arms for their country, myths that had prevailed among military leaders despite the fact that blacks had fought heroically in all of America's wars. Adams might also have known about a 1925 U.S. Army War College memo titled "The Use of Negro Man Power in War," which concluded, "The black man was physically unqualified for combat duty [and] was by nature subservient, mentally inferior, and believed himself to be inferior to the white man [and] was susceptible to the influence of crowd psychology, could not control himself in the face of danger, and did not have the initiative and resourcefulness of the white man."

2. The U.S. Army did not acknowledge the effect that racism could have on its troops' willingness to fight until Vietnam, when, as we will see in chapters 8 and 9, the radio broadcasts Clarence Adams beamed at African American soldiers in Vietnam may have heightened the military's awareness of the negative effects of racism on both black and white soldiers. During the Korean War some military leaders did urge that blacks be slowly integrated into white units, but often for the wrong reasons. Basing their arguments on long-standing historical myths, these proponents were convinced that all-black units were incapable of fighting courageously and effectively unless their alleged social and psychological shortcomings were overcome by the leadership of white soldiers and officers. See T. R. Fehrenbach, *This Kind of War: The Classic Korean War History* (1963; reprint, Washington, D.C.: Brassey's, 1998), 357–59.

3. What undoubtedly saved Clarence Adams's life and the lives of many other prisoners captured in November and December 1950 was the Chinese plan to keep their prisoners alive to exploit later for political purposes.

3. CAPTURED!

1. Two Korean War combat physicians and POWs, Sidney Esensten and William Shadish, believe the fatality rate for Americans captured in the last six months of 1950 to be much higher than the official figures. Esensten puts the figure at 75 percent (Sidney Esensten, "Memories of Life as a POW 35 Years Later," *The Graybeards* [July–August 1997]: 6), and Shadish at more than 65 percent (interview with editor, March 17, 2004).

4. CAMP 5

1. A copy of this letter appeared in the Chinese propaganda pamphlet "United Nations P.O.W.'s in Korea."

2. Years later, fellow prisoner Jim Crombie, who was white and certainly not a Progressive, acknowledged his gratitude to Clarence Adams: "When I first arrived [in Camp 5] . . . , Clarence Adams really helped me. He was a short, stocky, very personable guy. He really gave me a hand, asking what he could do to help." Lewis H. Carlson, *Remembered Prisoners of a Forgotten War* (New York: St. Martin's, 2002), 208.

3. For the last eighteen months of the war, the issue of repatriation was the major obstacle to achieving a cease-fire agreement. Either because of choice or Allied persuasion, thousands of North Korean and Chinese prisoners did not want to be repatriated to their Communist homelands. During these protracted negotiations, the possibility that some UN prisoners might also choose not to return home was not considered, at least by the American negotiators.

5. TURNCOAT?

1. Originally, twenty-three Americans refused repatriation, but two changed their mind and returned to the United States before the others left for China. Claude Batchelor and Edward Dickenson were each given dishonorable discharges and sentenced to long prison terms.

2. "Korean Puzzle: Americans Who Stay," *U.S. News and World Report*, October 9, 1953, 38–40.

3. "The Sorriest Bunch," *Newsweek*, February 8, 1954, 40.

4. Quoted in Harold Lavine, "Twenty-one G.I.s Who Chose Tyranny: Why They Left the U.S. for Communism," *Commentary*, July 1954, 41–46. Incidentally, none of the twenty-one came from New York City.

5. *Chicago Defender*, January 2, 1954.

6. *Pittsburgh Courier*, January 2, 1954.

7. "Korean Puzzle: Americans Who Stay," *U.S. News & World Report*, October 9, 1952, 38.

8. Adam J. Zweiback provides a comprehensive and incisive analysis of the popular reaction to the twenty-one Americans who chose not to be repatriated in his essay "The 21 Turncoat GIs: Nonrepatriations and the Political Culture of the Korean War," *The Historian* (Winter 1998): 342–62.

9. *Memphis Commercial Appeal*, April 15, 1954. In many ways, Victor Riesel's words anticipated Richard Condon's 1959 novel *The Manchurian Candidate*, which in 1962 John Frankenheimer turned into his blockbuster film of the same name. Both the novel and the film focused on brainwashed American POWs who were programmed to commit dastardly crimes against their own countrymen.

10. *U.S. News & World Report*, October 9, 1953, 39–40.

11. *Memphis Press-Scimitar*, September 24, 1953.

12. The American Broadcasting Corporation sponsored this effort to get the twenty-one to change their minds. The Veterans of Foreign Wars offered to send the recordings to Korea, although there is no evidence that these appeals were ever broadcast in Korea. Ibid., October 1, 1953.

13. Although Batchelor initially received a life sentence, this was reduced to twenty years and then to four and a half years. Batchelor was released from prison on March 18, 1959.

14. This letter appeared in Batchelor's court-martial files and is quoted in Raymond B. Lech, *Broken Soldiers: American Prisoners of War in North Korea* (Urbana: University of Illinois Press, 2000), 267.

6. UNIVERSITY DAYS

1. Lu Xun (1881–1936) was the pen name for Zhou Shuren. This quotation is from the preface to his *Call to Arms (Na Han)*, which was first published in 1922. The Foreign Languages Press of Beijing, for whom Clarence Adams once worked, published an English-language edition in 2000.

7. MARRIAGE AND FAMILY

1. Della Adams tells of a Wuhan schoolmate of her father's trying to contact him in the United States. Unfortunately, Clarence Adams had already died, but the old schoolmate insisted on coming to Memphis to visit Della and Lin. When he arrived, he told them, "I came because I had to meet the children of Adams and take photos of them back to Wuhan University for our class reunion this coming summer." The last thing he said to Della was, "Your father was a wonderful man and certainly our favorite among the American students."

8. THE FOREIGN LANGUAGES PRESS, AFRICANS, AND THE VIETNAM BROADCASTS

1. Upon their arrival back in the United States in July 1955, William Cowart, Lewis Griggs, and Otho Bell were immediately arrested and put in a stockade at Fort Baxter, San Francisco. Four months later they were released when a civilian court determined that the U.S. Army no longer had jurisdiction over them because in January 1954, Secretary of Defense Charles Wilson had ordered all twenty-one non-repatriates to be dishonorably discharged. Another eight of the twenty-one had returned home by 1958. After Clarence Adams returned in 1966, only Howard Adams and James Veneris remained in China. The one British marine who had refused repatriation had also returned to England.

2. Under the headline "Korean War Defector, as 'Voice' of Hanoi, Bids G.I.'s Get Out,"

the *New York Times* of August 15, 1965, referred to Clarence Adams as "the Vietnam version of Tokyo Rose," and quoted him saying to African American soldiers: "You G.I.'s are fighting people in Vietnam like the ones I fought in Korea. . . . Fellows, are you on the right side on this? The Vietnamese are not bombing your churches and killing your children. You are in the wrong battle here. You are fighting the wrong war. Brothers, go home. The Negro people need you back there."

9. GOING HOME!

1. The May 26, 1966, *New York Times* stated simply that Adams was returning home because he wanted to see his mother.
2. "Turncoat Admits Doing Propaganda Broadcasts," UPI dispatch, quoted in the *Memphis Press-Scimitar*, May 27, 1966.
3. Ibid.
4. This quote appeared in "Turncoat Denies He Was Ever a Communist," *New York Times*, July 5, 1966.

10. RECRIMINATIONS

1. The *Memphis Commercial Appeal* carried Ryskind's syndicated column on July 10, 1966.
2. *Memphis Press-Scimitar*, June 8, 1966.
3. Ibid., July 23, 1966.
4. Morris R. Wills as told to J. Robert Moskin, *Turncoat: An American's Twelve Years in Communist China* (Englewood Cliffs, N.J.: Prentice-Hall, 1966).
5. In January 1954, Secretary of Defense Charles Wilson ordered the U.S. Army to dishonorably discharge the twenty-one soldiers who had chosen China over repatriation. When in July 1955 three of the twenty-one, William Cowart, Lewis Griggs, and Otho Bell, returned to the United States, the army immediately imprisoned them on charges of collaboration. In November, a civilian court overruled the army, stating that it had forfeited its jurisdiction when it dishonorably discharged these men after they defected, thus making them civilians. See Lech, *Broken Soldiers*, 259–60.
6. Another reason for the committee's reluctance to put Clarence Adams on public display was that radicals like Jerry Rubin had turned the public hearings into a circus, including wild demonstrations and guerrilla theater in the streets and inside the crowded hearing room itself, all the while Clarence Adams was being privately questioned in a side chamber. Adding to the confusion, District Court judge Howard F. Corcoran ordered the committee to stop holding hearings under the separation of powers doctrine. The committee announced that it would defy the order, but when demonstrations again disrupted the proceedings and threatened to make a farce of the hearings, the committee terminated the proceedings without ever calling Adams to testify in public. See *Washington Post*, August 16–20, 1966.